SIMPLE
TROMPE L'OEIL

SIMPLE
TROMPE L'OEIL

20 STYLISH PROJECTS USING STENCILS AND FAUX FINISHES

MARY MACCARTHY
PHOTOGRAPHY BY GEOFF DANN

FIREFLY BOOKS

A FIREFLY BOOK

Published by Firefly Books Ltd., 2001

First Printing

Library of Congress Cataloguing in Publication Data is available.

National Library of Canada Cataloguing in Publication Data

MacCarthy, Mary (Mary Lisa Grania)
Simple trompe l'oeil : 20 projects using stencils and faux finishes

Includes index.
ISBN 1-55209-636-X (bound) ISBN 1-55209-634-3 (pbk.)

1. Stencil work. 2. Trompe l'oeil painting. I. Title.

TT270.M32 2001 745.7'3 C2001-930410-2

Published in Canada in 2001 by
Firefly Books Ltd.
3680 Victoria Park Avenue
Willowdale, Ontario M2H 3K1

Published in the United States in 2001 by
Firefly Books (U.S.) Inc.
P.O. Box 1338, Ellicott Station
Buffalo, New York 14205

First published in the United Kingdom in 2001 by
Cico Books Ltd.
32 Great Sutton Street London EC1V 0NB

Projects on pages 28–31 and 100–103 by Eri Heilijgers

Photography by Geoff Dann
Designed by Sara Kidd
Edited by Alison Wormleighton
Reproduction by Alliance Graphics, Singapore
Printed and bound in Singapore by Tien Wah Press

For Samuel and Rose with love

Contents

Techniques

Beginning Trompe
   l'Oeil Stenciling   6

Using Paints and Varnishes   8

Painting with Stencils   10

Projects

Delft Tiles   12

Card Table   16

Fire Screen   22

Marquetry Tray   28

Scagliola Table   32

Bamboo Chair   38

Ribbon Mirror   42

3-D Floor   46

Simple Mural   50

French Plate   56

Kilim Rug   60

Bathroom Cabinet   66

Texan Chest   72

Desk Box   78

Indian Print Blind   82

Stenciled Curtain   86

Key Cupboard   94

Gothic Frieze   100

Garden Basket   104

Window Box   110

Templates   114

Beginning trompe l'oeil stenciling

Trompe l'oeil utilizes three-dimensional effects and other paint techniques to create the illusion (literally, to "trick the eye") that the painted subject is real. When it involves only freehand painting, it can be daunting, but with stenciling as a basis for the trompe l'oeil, it becomes much simpler. The templates in this book give you a huge head start, because the basic design elements are already in place and ready to be transferred to whatever surface you wish to use. With these templates, and your own hand-painting to add some of the details or faux ("false") finishes like woodgrain, you will be able to produce surprisingly realistic-looking work. Even people who claim to have no artistic talent will gain the confidence to tackle elaborate projects.

Combining stenciling with hand-painting gives you the best of both worlds. When, for example, a number of repeat patterns are involved, a stencil will avoid a lot of tedious repetition, whether you are painting lots of little boxes or one large wall. Stencils are also handy when you are working on a symmetrical subject, as you stencil only half of the design and then turn the stencil over and paint the other side, thus ensuring that both halves are

ABOVE *The outer margin of a stencil is sometimes used as an aid to positioning.*

identical. Yet another attraction of stenciling is the fact that it gives crisp, sharp edges combined with a wonderful, subtle texture that is absolutely unique.

Initial preparation

Although pre-cut stencils are widely available, you will need to cut your own in order to do the projects in this book or to create your own designs. It is not difficult. Stencils can be cut from either oiled manila card or acetate. Card doesn't slip, is easy to draw on and cut out, and is long-lasting. Acetate, which is see-through, allows a template to be traced straight onto it and is also easy to position, but is more difficult to cut out. Card is shown throughout this book, but you can use whichever you prefer.

Prior to cutting a stencil, you need to plan the design, experiment with colors and decide on details and patterns, as well as measure the space you intend to stencil and work out the dimensions of the stencil. A sketch drawn to scale can be helpful in this planning stage. Once you are happy with all the elements, draw it up full-size as a template. If you are planning a big project where there is a large repeat pattern of one section, draw up just that section.

With some designs, you may simply have a separate stencil for each motif, while with others you may need to use overlays. These involve stenciling some of the elements of a motif, using one stencil, then placing a second

BELOW *The cut-out portion of a stencil can often be used to make a stencil for detailing.*

stencil over the top (after the paint has dried) and stenciling further elements, often in different colors.

Templates for many of the projects are at the back of the book. You can use them just as they are, or adapt them, but most will have to be enlarged. The easiest way to do this is on a photocopier. You may have to tape several copies together if the stencil is large.

If you don't have access to a photocopier, you can enlarge the design using the traditional grid method. With a ruler, draw a grid of about six to eight equal-sized squares each way on the template that is to be enlarged. Now measure out the required finished size on a piece of paper (allowing extra for a margin all around – see below), and draw a grid with the same number of squares on it. Finally, draw the design, square by square, on the paper.

Transferring a design

For an acetate stencil, trace the template using a felt-tip pen onto the non-shiny side of the acetate. Because you stencil from the shiny side, the image will be reversed. If you wish to avoid reversing it, place the template under glass and lay the acetate, shiny side up, over it, then cut the stencil.

To transfer a template onto stencil card, trace it onto good-quality tracing paper using a very soft (6B) pencil. Lay the tracing paper, penciled side down, on the stencil card, and secure it with a little masking tape, leaving a margin all around (see below). Using a hard (H) or medium (HB) pencil, draw firmly over the traced lines. The lines will be transferred faintly onto the stencil card. Draw over them before cutting out the stencil. Because the original, traced image is reversed after it has been transferred, you'll need to turn the stencil over. The good thing about this method is that it familiarizes you with the design, giving you a final chance to adjust it before cutting. When transferring the template to stencil card or acetate, allow a margin of at least 1¼in (3cm), and preferably about 2in (5cm), all around the edge. Without the margin, the stencil would not be strong enough; also, the margin helps prevent paint from smudging over the edge.

Sometimes the margin will need to be a particular width, to help with positioning – the outer edge can then be lined up with another edge, such as a previously stenciled motif, baseboard (skirting board), window, cornice, ceiling or penciled guide line.

ABOVE *The cut-out portion of a stencil can also be used to create a pattern within a pattern.*

Registration marks

These are notches or holes sometimes cut in stencils to allow accurate positioning of repeat motifs or overlays. They are not necessary in acetate stencils, as you can see the positioning through the acetate.

Cutting a stencil

Once you have transferred the template, place the card or acetate on a cutting mat. Practice cutting on a spare piece of card or acetate until you have mastered the technique. Use a craft knife with a small, very sharp, disposable blade – a Stanley knife is too clumsy, while the long blade on a scalpel (mat knife) is unwieldy. Change the blade frequently to keep it sharp.

Start cutting near the center of the stencil, and, where possible, cut the smaller windows (as the shapes you are cutting out are called) before the larger ones, so as not to weaken the stencil while you are cutting it. Hold the knife like a pencil in an upright position in your right hand (or left if you are left-handed). Use your other hand to hold the stencil, always keeping that hand behind the knife and out of the cutting path. Press the blade into the stencil and pull it firmly toward you, making sure that your arm is on the table and your hand is free to move. As soon as it becomes awkward, move the stencil to a better position and continue cutting, so that you are always in control of the knife. If possible, try to cut a curve with a single stroke so that it is smooth.

Hints

If you accidentally cut through a bridge, don't panic. Just patch it up with a sliver of masking tape stuck on each side of the stencil.

Many of the projects in this book require the use of the inner, cut-out portions of the stencils, so don't throw these away. They may be used for stenciling details, such as the veins on the leaves in the Garden Basket or for creating patterns within patterns, such as on the Kilim Rug. They are also handy for masking off a shape while stenciling another one close to it.

Using paints and varnishes

Water-based products are used wherever possible in this book. Quick-drying and non-toxic, they are very easy to work with.

Types of paint

Artist's acrylic paints are used for nearly every project. They are ideal for stenciling, because, being water-based, they are quick-drying and waterproof when dry. They can be used in a thick or a thin consistency and also cover well, which is particularly important for trompe l'oeil.

The base coats used for projects are mainly latex (emulsion) paint, which is also water-based and dries quickly. It can be used for stenciling large areas, as it is less expensive than acrylic. Its drawback is that it is more liable to mark, but you can protect the base coat if you wish by applying a coat of clear matte latex (emulsion) glaze, which works like a weak water-based varnish, before stenciling. For wood surfaces, a dead flat, oil-based paint, can be used as a base coat and stenciled over with acrylic paint. To improve adhesion, converting primer can be used if desired.

Paint consistency

Acrylic paint is more or less the right consistency as it comes out of the tube, but if it is too dry and powdery-looking when stenciled, you could thin it a tiny bit. Adding a drop or two of clear matte medium produces a more translucent, flexible paint without making it too thin and watery. However, a drop of water can be used instead, so long as you don't make it too runny, which would cause it to bleed under the edges of the stencil windows, creating fuzzy edges and spots. The ideal consistency is slightly sticky, and with practice you will learn to recognize when it is right.

For glazes (see page 10), a higher proportion of matte medium is used.

Colors of paint

When mixing colors, start with very small quantities. Squeeze the paint onto one side of your palette – a paper plate works well – and mix it with a palette knife. Now slide some of the paint away from the main blob to dab the brush in; this will help prevent you from loading your brush with too much paint. Usually only three colors are needed at one time. For example, you might use alizarin crimson, toned down with raw umber, and made paler with unbleached titanium.

Once you have created the shade you want, mix enough for the whole job, so that you won't have to match the color halfway through. If it is a large project, you will need to put it in a jam jar with a lid. If you miscalculate and have to mix some more paint, do so before the first batch has run out, to allow you to compare the colors while wet.

Of course, it is sometimes fun to break all the rules and use bright colors. With this type of project, you can feel free to use whatever colors you like, and forgetting subtlety.

LEFT *Muted shades of gray and cream can have as much impact as strong colors.*

ABOVE *This marquetry-effect project uses a combination of opaque paint (to provide the background), translucent glaze (to create the faux woodgrain), and varnish (to fix the color, bring out the woodgrain texture and protect the surface).*

Varnishes

Varnishing not only protects your work but also enhances colors. It is essential for surfaces that will receive wear and tear, such as table tops. When a tinted varnish is used (tinted, say, with raw sienna and black, or with Payne's gray), it can miraculously "age" the paint and soften the look of the piece. Most of the projects use a clear, matte, water-based varnish, sometimes called acrylic varnish. Very easy to use, it dries quickly, and so two or three coats can be applied in a day.

For floors, use a special, extra-hard water-based varnish formulated for floors. For outdoor projects, such as the Garden Basket and the Window Box (pages 104 and 110), use an exterior varnish like yacht varnish. This is oil-based and so will yellow slightly over time, but it is extremely hard-wearing and waterproof.

When varnishing, you must use a special brush (see page 11). Wear cotton clothing rather than wool, and keep the area clean and as dust-free as possible by vacuuming an hour or so beforehand to give any dust time to settle. Stir the varnish well, and dip the brush in only halfway up the bristles. Apply the varnish swiftly and steadily. Do not go back over it or the surface will become rough and cloudy. Any missed areas can be covered with the second coat. Two or three coats should be enough. Always allow each coat to dry completely before applying the next.

Hint

Most of the projects use similar colors, which can be divided into four main categories: primary colors (Turner's yellow, Naples yellow, cadmium red, permanent rose, alizarin crimson, ultramarine, cobalt, cerulean blue); secondary colors (prism violet, Hooker's green, chromium oxide green, aqua green); neutral colors (titanium white, black, Payne's gray, unbleached titanium); and earth colors (raw umber, raw sienna, burnt umber, burnt sienna, ocher, red oxide). Using the same earth colors to mix with the primaries and secondaries creates a softly toning, harmonious overall effect if you do more than one project.

BELOW *Two primary colors (permanent rose and Turner's yellow) and a secondary color (aqua green) are used together on this mirror frame.*

Painting with stencils

Hint

Clean your brushes thoroughly after use. For water-based paints and varnishes, use warm water and dishwashing (washing-up) liquid; for oil-based ones, use mineral spirits (white spirit) and a brush cleaner. Leave the brushes to dry in the air before using them again. To keep them in good shape, wrap newspaper around the hair, securing it with a rubber band.

Trompe l'oeil stenciling involves stenciling the basic shapes and, sometimes, the decoration, then filling in the gaps left by the stencil bridges and painting additional fine details by hand. Finally, a three-dimensional effect is created using shading and highlighting.

Brushes and brush strokes

There are several types of brush you will need, each in a variety of sizes. Whenever you are buying any brush, always feel the hair, which should be soft and flexible. Coarse-haired brushes leave unattractive streaks in the paint.

Household paintbrushes are used for applying undercoats and base coats. Three sizes – 1½in (3.7cm), 2in (5cm), and 3in (8cm) – will cover most jobs, though for large wall-painting jobs, a 5in (13cm) brush is quicker.

A stencil brush has a round "stock" with flat-cut bristles. Avoid hard-bristled brushes, as the paint does not slide off so well. Older, softer brushes are often the best. Try to keep one for every color – it is more convenient and it keeps your colors clear.

Choose stencil brushes that are slightly bigger than you think you need; large ones leave a softer, smoother brush stroke and you don't have to dip them in paint so often. Buy about three small ones, ¼–⅜in (6mm–1cm); three

medium ones, ⅜–⅝in (1–1.5cm); and three large ones, ¾–2in (2–5cm). You will probably use the 1⅜in (3.5cm) and ⅝in (1.5cm) brushes the most.

The stencil brush should be just barely damp; if it is wet, you will have the same problems of bleeding as when the paint is too thin. To test whether your brush is too wet prior to taking up the paint, squeeze the tip. If it froths up, dry the brush on a paper towel. Overloading the brush with paint will give the stenciling an unpleasant, heavy look, so allow the paint to go only ¼in (6mm) up the bristles, and work it in well.

Hold a stencil brush like a pencil, but upright. For most stenciling, use a loose, swirling action, starting at the edges of each stencil window so that the color will be softer at the center. Sometimes, however, a project specifies a stippling action. For narrow stencil windows, use either stippling or back-and-forth brush strokes.

A collection of artist's brushes is essential for the fine work that characterizes trompe l'oeil, such as over-painting stencils, filling in the gaps left by stencil bridges, detailing, shading, and highlighting. The most useful artist's brush is a fine (No. 2), fairly long-bristled acrylic brush, because it holds the paint well and the hairs fall into a good point. Acrylic or polyester brushes are particularly compatible with acrylic paint. Sable brushes, although expensive, are very smooth and will last a long time if well looked after. To hand-paint with an artist's brush, relax your hand and shoulder. Steady your hand with your little finger and support your wrist.

Lining brushes, or liners, are used to paint lines, but they can also sometimes be substituted for artist's brushes. When painting straight lines, rest your little finger against the edge of the work or against a ruler, and glide your hand downward with a confident, steady speed, and even pressure.

Stenciling the basic shapes

Make sure the surface to be stenciled is clean and fairly smooth. If it is gloss-painted, sand it to provide a "key" so that the paint will adhere. Remove any varnish or wax. Paint on the base coat if there is to be one (normally two coats are necessary), allowing it to dry after each coat. Depending on the project, you may need to mark out the parameters of the design on the space you are stenciling, particularly if it is a

BELOW *Soft, light shadows are applied as a glaze using a large brush on this trompe l'oeil curtain.*

ABOVE *Neatly filling in the gaps left by stencil bridges is a key stage in trompe l'oeil stenciling.*

large area of wall. Do this in pencil or charcoal. Think about where you will start stenciling – for example, you may need to center it on, say, a chimney front.

Fix the stencil to the wall with spray adhesive or low-tack masking tape, which will be less likely than ordinary tape to pull off the underlying paint. Mask any areas that need to be protected, using either masking tape or a cut-out portion of the stencil. Mix the paint, pick it up with the brush and stencil with it. Reposition the stencil as appropriate, being careful to allow the paint to dry first if you are using an overlay stencil or are overlapping it.

Check whether any paint has crept onto the underside of the stencil, and wipe it off with a paper towel so that it won't smudge onto the surface. Try not to let paint build up around the edges of the stencil windows, or it could prevent the stenciled image from being crisp and sharp. When the paint is dry, carefully remove any tape that was used for masking, pulling it gently back on itself.

Detailing

The decoration may be stenciled too, often as stencils cut from the portion removed from the main stencil, or it may be applied by hand with a fine artist's brush or liner. Make sure that the stenciling is dry before starting on this. The bridges, which are the characteristic feature of conventional stenciling, have to be filled in using a fine artist's brush.

Shading and highlighting

This is what will make your painting look three-dimensional and realistic. Some shading is actually done with the stenciling, either by leaving the center pale and concentrating the paint on the edges, or by stenciling a stronger or darker ocher around the edges. However, additional shadows can be added separately, in the form of a glaze – a mixture of matte medium and a minute amount of acrylic in raw umber and Payne's gray (or similar). The glaze needs to be quite thin and translucent so that the stencilings underneath are still visible. If necessary, you can add a drop of water, too, to help the mixture glide off the brush. Some shadows will be quite strong and dark, as if a bright sun were shining onto the object. For these, add extra Payne's gray and a touch of black. In other instances, only a suggestion of shadow is appropriate, so for these you should add more medium.

The shadows are occasionally ocher but are more often hand-painted. Thin, dark shadows, applied with a fine brush, should follow the shape of the object. Some shadows, though, are light gray, soft and relaxed; they are applied with a large, soft brush that has a good point. The direction of the light must be the same for each shadow that you add to a particular project.

Whenever there are shadows, there are also highlights, though these are often very subtle. Acrylic paint is used for highlights, and as these paints are much more opaque, just a touch of white paint will often be sufficient. Think carefully which part of the object you are painting would catch the light.

BELOW *To create a realistic effect, shadows are essential.*

This panel of tiles mimics the famous Delft designs which were extremely popular throughout the 19th century. The simple repeating pattern is ideal in a

Delft Tiles

kitchen but would be equally suitable for a bathroom, and can be painted on either the wall or a board. The size of the tiles and panel can be adjusted to suit the space. It is also far quicker – and cleaner – to stencil a tile panel than try to create a real one!

YOU WILL NEED

Sheet of ¼in (6mm) MDF or wall

Latex (emulsion) paint: white

Stencils: square, corner motif, tulip, pink (dianthus)

Matte medium

Acrylic paint: raw umber, titanium white, Payne's gray, prism violet, alizarin crimson, red oxide

Brushes: household paintbrush; medium and large stencil brushes; 1/0 liner; varnishing brush

Semi-gloss varnish

1 Using the household paintbrush, paint the surface with two coats of white latex (emulsion); allow to dry. Now, with the large stencil brush and the square stencil, apply a light background color to each tile. Use three slightly different, very light mixtures for this – raw umber mixed with white; Payne's gray mixed with white; and a mixture of the other two – to create the impression of age while ensuring that the differences remain subtle. Don't forget to leave narrow gaps between the tiles for the "grout" (mortar).

2 Mix plenty of matte medium and a little water with raw umber, prism violet, Payne's gray, and alizarin crimson to create a soft manganese color. Using a medium stencil brush and the corner-motif stencil, paint the corners, again varying the shade slightly for each tile. Don't worry if the motifs do not fit exactly into the corners.

3 Stencil the flowers with the same paint, using the medium stencil brush, the tulip stencil and the pink (dianthus) stencil, and alternating the two designs.

Hint

When stenciling the tiles, remember that the originals – made in Delft in the 17th century – were all produced by hand, so each has its own individuality. When you hand-paint the finishing touches, don't worry about ensuring that each tile is identical. In fact, a wobbly line of grout or an extra dark shadow on a corner will make the whole design seem more authentic.

4 Add more raw umber to the soft manganese color used in steps 2–3; apply this with the liner to outline and define each of the tulip and pink (dianthus) motifs. Add dots to the pink (dianthus) petals, lines to separate the tulip petals, extra lines at the base of each petal, and more fronds around the base of each flower.

5 Use the liner to paint lines of grout between the tiles in a very light mix of red oxide, raw umber, and white. When dry, mix Payne's gray with white and some matte medium, and hand-paint a thin gray line around the edge of each tile, using the liner. Don't worry about the uneven edges of the tiles – this adds to their handmade appearance.

6 Add further authenticity to the tiles with a few "age cracks", using a liner and a very light mix of raw umber and glaze. Also add a few spots and dots across the face of the tile.

7 To finish, "dirty up" the corners of the tiles using the same mixture of raw umber and glaze as in step 6, scuffing the paint very softly onto the edges of the tiles with the large stencil brush. As well as "aging" the tiles, this will help "raise" the tile away from the grout groove. To protect the surface and give the panel the sheen of real tiles, apply a coat of semi-gloss varnish. (For a slightly bluish tinge, tint it first with a little Payne's gray.)

A small games table with a half-finished card game and a row of dominoes helps to create a family atmosphere and to give a room that vital feeling of warmth. Choose your favorite card game and have fun stenciling the overlapping

Card Table

YOU WILL NEED
Small wooden table

Latex (emulsion) paint: rusty red

Water-based matte and semi-matte varnish; matte medium

Stencils (see steps 1, 2, 4, and 7): card shape, suits, card-back, domino shape, edges, dots

Acrylic paint: black, titanium white, cadmium red, Hooker's green, raw sienna, raw umber, Payne's gray

Brushes: medium household paint-brush; medium artist's brush; small, medium, and large stencil brushes; 1/0 liner; varnishing brush

Holepuncher, pencil

playing cards scattered on the table – they look so real that you will almost feel like picking them up and continuing the game. Nearly all the elements of this project are stenciled, from the shadows of the cards and the patterns of dots on the dominoes to the cards lying on top of each other in the center of the table, so it is easy to re-create even the most complicated of games.

1 Using a medium household paintbrush, apply two coats of rusty red latex (emulsion) paint to the table. When dry, apply a coat of matte water-based varnish to protect it. Allow to dry. Paint the rim and legs with black acrylic, using a medium artist's brush, again applying two coats. (You can mask the edges if you are not confident about hand-painting straight lines.) Plan the design, overlapping some of the cards – remember that they should not look tidy and regimented. Stencil the card shapes in white, using a large stencil brush. (The easiest way to make a stencil for the cards is simply to draw around a real playing card on stencil card, then cut it out. Save the cut-out portion to use for masking later.) When dry, stencil a second coat. Leave to dry.

2 Now stencil the suit symbols on the white card shapes, using a large stencil brush. (The suit motifs for the stencils can be taken from actual cards.) Use black for the Clubs and Spades, and cadmium red for the Hearts and Diamonds. Do not stencil the numbers.

3 Trace the numbers and transfer them to the cards, then use a 1/0 liner to hand-paint them in black or red, to match the suit symbols. While wobbly hand-painting is normally acceptable, even desirable, in most stenciling projects, here the aim is to look uniformly printed.

4 Stencil the backs of the playing cards in a mixture of Hooker's green, white, and raw sienna, using a medium stencil brush and protecting any overlapping cards as in step 5. (The stencil for the back of the cards can be taken from the template at the back of the book or from your own cards.)

5 When you are stenciling two playing cards that overlap, stencil the underneath card first, while masking the uppermost card with the cut-out portion of the card-shape stencil. Then remove the cut-out piece and, when the paint on the underneath card is dry, stencil the uppermost card. (When you are overlapping more than two cards, you will not necessarily need to cover up all the cards – just any cards that fall within the stencil area.)

Style Ideas

If you are feeling confident about your hand-painting skills, you could trace one or more of the court cards (Jack, Queen and King) from a deck of cards. Transfer the design(s) to the white stenciled cards and then hand-paint them using the liner brush and more colors.

Style Ideas

The shadows will look more realistic if you make them consistent with the direction of the actual light in the room, which depends on where the table will be placed relative to the windows.

6 The shadows around the cards are important. Mix raw umber and Payne's gray together, diluting the mixture to a thin consistency with matte medium and water, and then use the liner to carefully hand-paint a narrow line around two edges of each card. You will need to decide which direction the light appears to come from, and always put the shadow on the same two sides on each card. On the table shown here, it is the left and bottom edges that are shaded. Also use the liner to hand-paint a few bent or torn edges, to add further realism. When the cards are completely dry, use the medium stencil brush to paint a thin wash of raw sienna over them to make them look old.

7 With the small stencil brush and the rectangular domino stencil, paint the domino shapes in a mixture of black, a little white, and raw umber. Leave until completely dry. Using the dots stencils (made by using a holepuncher), stencil white dots with the small stencil brush.

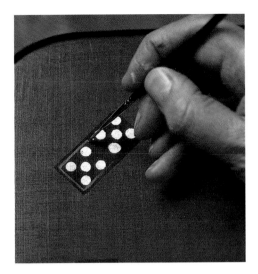

8 Continue stenciling white dots, making sure they are in the correct order for a real game of dominoes. Leave some of the dominoes without dots (see main photograph). With the liner, paint a black line just inside two edges of each domino; these should be on the same sides as the playing-card shadows. Paint a line in Payne's gray inside the other two edges.

9 Using the stencil for the domino edges, paint the edges and the ridge between the two halves black. For the dominoes that don't have white dots, stencil the edges in Payne's gray, and also stencil a diamond shape on the top in this color.

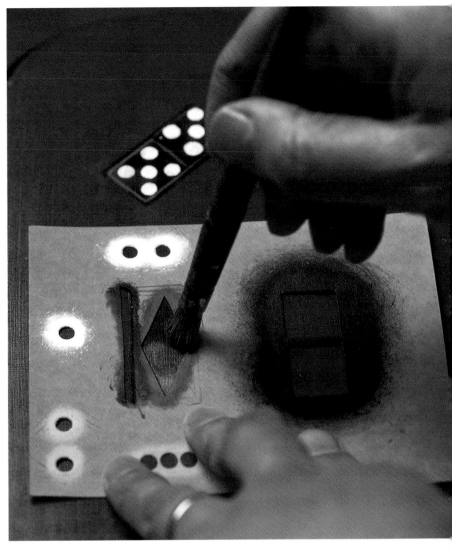

Style Ideas

Make up your own design for a card table, using other games such as Scrabble or Snakes & Ladders. Arranging real cards, dominoes, etc, on the table before starting is the easiest way to plan the design and this will also help make the paintwork look more like a real game. Another idea is to paint a single card, or perhaps a particularly good hand of cards on the mantelpiece.

10 With the same thin mixture as you used for the shadows cast by the playing cards in step 6, paint shadows along the same edges of the dominoes as for the playing cards. When all the paint is dry, apply two coats of semi-matte varnish to the table.

Appropriately for a fireplace, the 1st-century pottery vase from China depicted on this fire screen is glowing with warm color. The patterns on the vase, which were loosely hand-painted on the original vase in unfired pigments, are as

Fire Screen

appealing today as they were two thousand years ago. For a realistic effect, however, try to make the vase look antique, with paint chipped off in places to reveal the clay. The fire screen is not difficult to make. The main features are stenciled, and, as long as you take care to protect the areas you have just painted with masking tape or card, you should not have any trouble re-creating this stunning centerpiece.

YOU WILL NEED
Board to fit fireplace

Pencil, straightedge, masking tape

Latex (emulsion) paint: white, black

Stencils (see Hints): Chinese vase; fireback top; clay pot; lily stem/leaves, flower, buds, cane; bayleaf spray

Acrylic paint: titanium white, ocher, Naples yellow, raw umber, orange, Payne's gray, red oxide, burnt umber, Hooker's green, cadmium red

Brushes: household paintbrush; 1/0 liner; small and large stencil brushes; varnishing brush

Water-based varnish

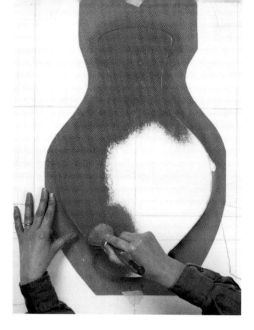

1 Using a household paintbrush, prime the board with two coats of white latex (emulsion); allow to dry thoroughly. Mix white, ocher, yellow, and raw umber together. Measure and mark the center of the board, and that of the vase stencil; place the stencil on the board, aligning center marks. Stencil it in this yellow background color, using a large stencil brush. Add a little raw umber to the yellow background color, and apply this around the sides as shading. Add a little orange to the original yellow, and apply around the base as more shading. Add a little white to the yellow, and apply in the middle as highlighting. Be free and painterly with the color.

2 Using a straightedge, pencil in the sides of the fireplace; mask with tape. Mask the stenciled vase with the cut-out portion of its stencil. Draw the fireback using its stencil. Position the cut-out portion as shown. Paint the background above and alongside it in black latex (emulsion), using the household paintbrush. Lift it off and reverse it, then paint the rest of the black background.

Hints

Save the cut-out parts of stencils; they often come in handy to use as masks when painting. Here the cut-out portions of the fireback top, Chinese vase, and clay pot have been used.

To create depth, use perspective, in which lines that in real life are parallel are drawn going toward each other a little, as in the fireplace floor.

3 With the masking tape and the stencil cut-outs still in place, paint the fireback in a dark gray mix of Payne's gray and white, using the household paintbrush. Add a little more white to the mix and paint the wall to the right of the fireback, as though the light were shining on it.

4 Add black emulsion to the dark gray, and paint the fireplace floor, gradually deepening the color as you work from the front to the back. Allow the board to dry and remove the masking tape. When dry, use the liner to paint thin gray grouting lines on the floor to indicate tiles (see diagram on p27).

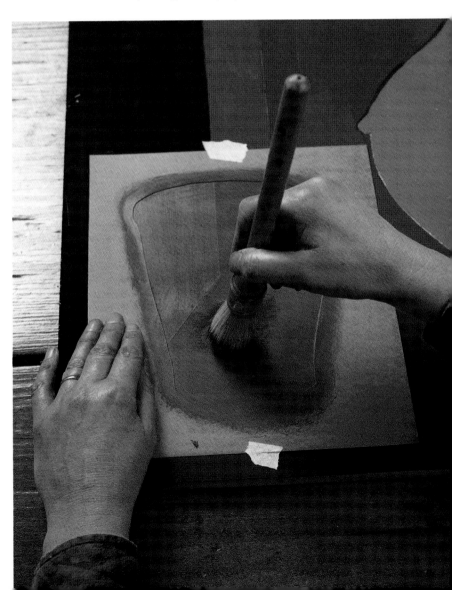

5 When dry, mask the vertical edges of the fireback, and tape the stencil for the top in place. Add more white to the dark gray, and, using the household paintbrush, paint the fireback, adding extra white for the top edge. Reverse the stencil to paint the remainder of the fireback top.

6 Stencil the clay pots on either side of the fireback with a mixture of white, red oxide, raw umber, and a little ocher, using a large stencil brush. Apply two or even three coats in order to prevent the black background from showing through.

7 Using the top edge of the cut-out portion of the stencil, cut a long oval. Tape it over the top of the stenciled pot. Paint the rim in a darker shade of red oxide and raw umber, using a small stencil brush. Begin shaping the pot, highlighting it with a mixture of white and a little ocher dabbed up and down the center with a large stencil brush. Shade the sides with raw umber, and scuff a little dry white paint over it. Remove the oval and paint the earth at the top of the pot in a dark mixture of burnt umber and Payne's gray. Remove the stencil. Repeat for the other pot.

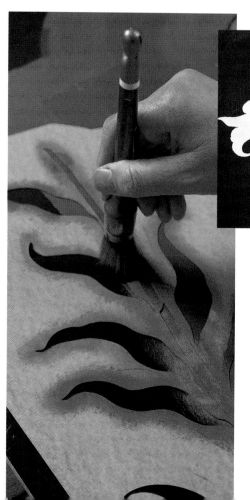

8 Stencil the lily stems and leaves with a dark mixture of Hooker's green, ocher, and white. Vary the shades for different leaves, but ensure that the background doesn't show through. Add darker green shading. When dry, stencil white flowers and buds along the length of the stem. The paint must be thick enough to cover the black or any leaves that fall underneath. With the liner, hand-paint veins and shading on the flowers and buds in a soft green and in Payne's gray.

9 Stencil the cane with a mixture of yellow, ocher, white, and a little raw umber. Place the cane so it will seem to fall behind some leaves but in front of others. Use small pieces of card to mask where leaves will overlap across the front of the cane. With the liner, hand-paint dark green ties.

10 Use the liner to neatly fill in the gaps on the lily stem and on the cane which have been left by the stencil bridges. Now carefully hand-paint the stamens on the lily flowers, using both yellow and orange, with green for the filaments.

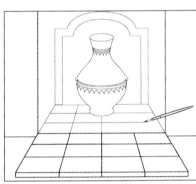

Style Ideas

The techniques used for painting the lilies can also be adapted for other types of flowers. For example, the bayleaf sprays in this project have been painted in the same way as the lily stems and leaves, but with brown stems and light green veins.

11 Paint the inside of the vase at the top with a mix of raw and burnt umber. Cut patterns in the cut-out part of the vase stencil. Stencil or hand-paint the decoration in shades of red (cadmium red mixed with raw umber) and brown (raw umber mixed with burnt umber).

12 Hand-paint a few brown chips with white edges. Scuff on a dry mix of raw and burnt umber with a large stencil brush. Mix a thin glaze of diluted raw umber and Payne's gray, and shade the sides. Stencil bayleaf sprays in the vase and on the floor, as in steps 8–10. Varnish.

The neoclassical wreath design of this stylish tray recreates a typical Biedermeier effect, a German and Austrian 19th-century style that is popular again today. Biedermeier surfaces often combine light-colored wood with ebony inlays, such as

Marquetry Tray

marquetry and other veneer decoration. A faux woodgrain can be surprisingly easy to create. For the tray shown here, the oval-shaped inset mimics maple, a wood much used in

Biedermeier style. The black stenciled wreath mimics ebony and the yellowish surroundings lemon wood (citronnier).

YOU WILL NEED
Wooden tray

Water-based eggshell paint: bright yellow

Oval cardboard template (see step 2)

Waterproof black felt-tip pen

Pigments in dry tempera or liquid poster paint: burnt sienna, burnt umber; stale beer (see step 3)

Brushes: medium household paintbrush; dragging brush; wavy mottler; medium stenciling brush; varnishing brush

Amber-colored oil-based varnish

Stencil: wreath

Acrylic paint: black

1 Using the household paintbrush, paint the bottom of the tray with a base coat of yellow water-based eggshell paint. If you're using different colors, remember that the base coat should be the lightest tone.

2 Make an oval template from cardboard, or ask a picture framer to cut one for you, to size. Position the oval in the center of the tray, and draw around it with a waterproof black felt-tip pen.

3 Mix a glaze of two parts burnt sienna to one part burnt umber, adding a little stale beer to help it adhere. Paint the oval with the glaze using a specialist brush known as a dragging brush in long, sweeping strokes (see Hints).

4 Immediately drag a wavy mottler (another specialist brush) across the surface from side to side in overlapping bands to create the maple grain. The undulating movement will produce darker areas where the glaze is concentrated.

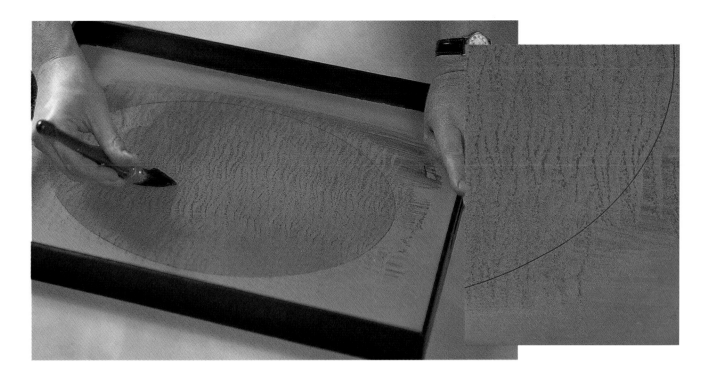

5 When the glaze is dry, cover the oval with an oil-based varnish. A yellow or amber-colored varnish will bring out the warmth of the wood. When dry, wipe away any glaze from outside the oval with a cloth dampened with spirits.

6 Center the wreath stencil over the woodgrained oval and use the medium stencil brush to apply black acrylic paint. Once dry, apply a second coat of the glaze from step 3 over the entire tray, including the bright yellow surroundings, using the dragging brush.

7 The extra layer of glaze willl make the "maple" oval a stronger color, emphasizing the contrast with what surrounds it. It will also warm up the yellow of this "citronnier" woodgrain effect. When the glaze is dry, cover the whole tray with the same oil-based varnish as in step 5.

Hints

A water-based glaze such as this one gives a more realistic finish than an oil-based glaze, but the fast drying time means you have to work quickly, and over only a small area such as a tray. When applying the glaze using a dragging brush to create the undergraining, make sure that all the brush strokes run in the direction of the grain, in this case along the length of the tray. Use long, sweeping strokes without stopping before the end.

Scagliola Table

Scagliola (pronounced "scalyola") is a technique for imitating costly inlaid marble, and this project convincingly imitates scagliola. The technique was much used in 18th-century Italy, when wonderful table tops and other pieces were created.

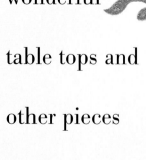

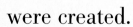

YOU WILL NEED
Table

Latex (emulsion) paint: graphite

Very fine steel wool

Matte medium

Stencils: scagliola design (lapis lazuli and grayish-purple/brown portions)

Acrylic paint: burnt umber, ultramarine, titanium white, raw umber, gold, prism violet, Payne's gray, raw sienna, Naples yellow, burnt sienna

Brushes: medium and large stencil brushes; fine artist's brush; varnishing brush

Matte water-based varnish

Hints

The design for the table top is produced with two overlay stencils covering just over one-quarter of the table. Trace the motif onto two pieces of stencil card and then cut the parts of the design that will be blue (which are mimicking lapis lazuli) out of one stencil and the remaining motifs out of the other. As the design is symmetrical in both directions, the stencils are used on all four corners of the table top (with the central motifs just stenciled once). Either stencil can be used first.

1 Use a large stencil brush in a swirling action to paint the table top in a graphite latex (emulsion). When dry, rub over the surface with very fine steel wool. Now rub a glaze of burnt umber and matte medium over it with a cloth. Leave to dry.

2 Place the "lapis lazuli" stencil so that the center of the top right-hand oval is at the exact center of the table top. Mix (but only slightly) ultramarine with a little white and raw umber. Using a medium stencil brush, stencil all the lapis lazuli motifs.

3 Without removing the stencil, use a fine artist's paintbrush to add dark spots and flecks (using the blue mixture but with less white added) and a little gold over the blue. Smudge the gold with your finger. Remove the stencil. If you wish, you can turn it over now to stencil the other quarters of the table top in the same way. Use the central motifs as a guide to positioning, but you obviously do not need to stencil them again. Alternatively, stencil the remainder in step 11.

4 Put the other stencil over the stenciled quarter. Unevenly mix raw umber, violet, Payne's gray, and white. With the medium stencil brush, stipple the border. You can do the central ring now or when you stencil the last quarter (step 11).

5 When the grayish purple stippled in step 4 is dry, you may need to apply a second coat in order to cover the dark base coat thoroughly. Now roughly mix raw sienna and Naples yellow, and, with a medium stencil brush, stencil the curled pattern of twining foliage.

6 Also use this mixture of raw sienna and Naples yellow, and the medium stencil brush, to stencil the motif that appears above the semicircle; this motif is only stenciled once on each long side of the table. Take care to stencil right into the sharp points. Remove the stencil.

7 Use a fine artist's brush and the same shades as in steps 4–6 to fill in the gaps left by the stencil bridges. Try to maintain the same textured effect.

Style Ideas

These clear, scroll-like patterns are very suitable for stencils, and the streaks and flecks that imitate scagliola are easy to do. In fact, inlaid scagliola and marble designs on antique furniture, particularly table tops, provide a wealth of design ideas for this type of trompe l'oeil. Look through books on 18th-century antiques, and trace some of the designs shown there, adapting the motifs as necessary.

8 With a fine artist's paintbrush, paint white streaks diagonally along the grayish purple border. They should all face roughly the same direction (i.e., at about the same angle as the end of the border at the corner), but should be quite jagged.

9 Mix a slightly darker version of the grayish purple shade that was used for the border in step 4, using less white this time. Paint small, uneven dots and smudges over the border with this, using a fine artist's paintbrush.

10 Still using a fine artist's brush, dot Naples yellow and burnt sienna on the stenciled brown parts of the design. If any of the gaps that you filled in by hand in step 7 are noticeable, these spots are useful for helping to camouflage them.

Style Ideas

This table has a stretcher running between the two wide legs, providing an excellent opportunity for repeating a small motif taken from the table top design. Look for suitable spots in the piece of furniture you are stenciling, and select a portion of the motif that is the right shape for the space. However, don't be tempted simply to fill all available space, unless you are seeking a heavily patterned effect. Remember that the background has an important role to play in setting off the design. When choosing colors, don't forget to take into account the room and particularly the accessories you will be placing on or near the project. Here, blue is the keynote.

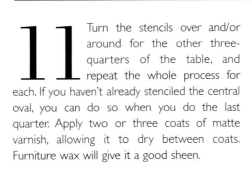

11 Turn the stencils over and/or around for the other three-quarters of the table, and repeat the whole process for each. If you haven't already stenciled the central oval, you can do so when you do the last quarter. Apply two or three coats of matte varnish, allowing it to dry between coats. Furniture wax will give it a good sheen.

Bamboo furniture became popular in the West during the 17th century. However, because it was so expensive to import from China, faux bamboo soon appeared, becoming highly fashionable in the 18th century. It still looks good today and is a

Bamboo Chair

good way of smartening up an old wooden chair, another item of furniture, or a picture frame. The bamboo color comes from a base coat of pale ocher, dead flat oil paint, while the black nodes and the dark "eyes" of the bamboo are hand-painted or stenciled. This is a fun project to work on, because faux bamboo always entails an element of whimsy and fantasy.

YOU WILL NEED
Wooden chair

Dead flat oil paint:
soft ocher

Straightedge, pencil

Masking tape

Stencils: circles in
two sizes

Acrylic paint: black,
ocher, raw sienna,
burnt sienna

Brushes: household
paintbrush; liner;
small stencil brush;
varnishing brush

Semi-matte water-
based varnish

Style Ideas

Make faux bamboo look even more authentic by building up mock nodes using plaster of Paris before painting. For each one, roll the plaster onto the dampened wood with your finger, then, when dry, smooth it with fine sandpaper and carve a groove around the center using a craft knife. Another technique for adding to the illusion is to drag a raw umber glaze over a pale yellow base coat.

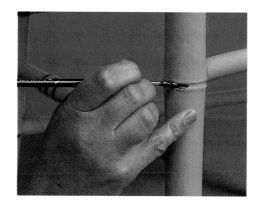

1 Paint the chair with two coats of soft ocher oil paint using the household paintbrush. When dry, use the liner to paint the grooves black.

2 Using a straightedge, pencil in the long straight lines that will be painted black on the edge of the seat and along the length of the rungs between the legs.

3 Using the liner and black acrylic, paint the lines on the rungs, following the pencil lines. Keep the lines as straight as possible, using masking tape if needed.

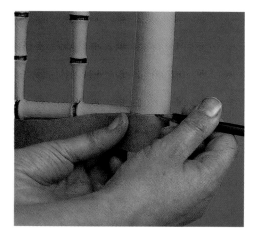

4 You can also add lines in the areas that are not turned. To keep the lines straight on the curved parts, such as the back, mask the lines and pencil along them.

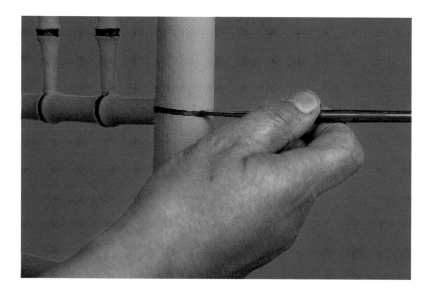

5 If you wish, you can leave the tape in place while you paint the black lines by hand, using the liner. Remember to carefully remove the tape afterward. The lines will match those around the seat and along the rungs better if you remove the tape before painting them. Paint black lines on the chair legs and back wherever horizontal cross-pieces, such as the rungs, meet these vertical pieces. Also paint them on the crosspieces of the back where the spindles meet them, and at "nodes" (whether on turned areas or on areas that aren't turned) on the spindles and rungs.

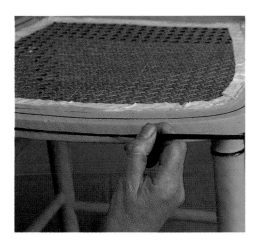

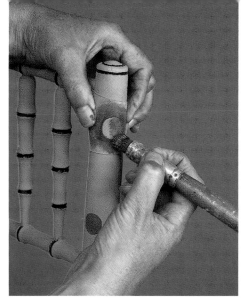

6 In the same way as in step 3, paint the long, thin, penciled line around the seat, using black acrylic paint and the liner, making the line as straight as possible.

7 Mix ocher and raw sienna, and stencil the outer portion of each round "eye" on the back and legs. When dry, stencil burnt sienna spots on top.

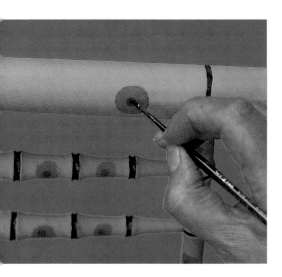

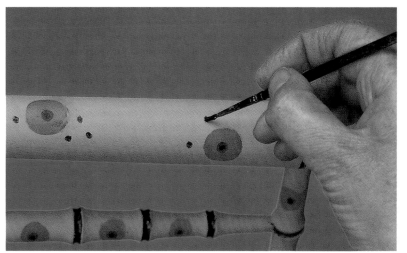

8 When the "eyes" that were stenciled in step 7 are dry, use the liner brush to hand-paint spots at the center of each one in black acrylic.

9 With the liner, hand-paint small dots grouped in threes around the "eyes." Also add an occasional spot where there are large empty spaces.

10 Finally, when the paint is completely dry, protect your paintwork by varnishing the chair. Use a semi-matte water-based varnish tinted with raw sienna and black to add an aged effect.

Realistic shading and highlighting make this frame look as though a length of ribbon really is folded around the mirror in a zigzag pattern. It would look lovely in a girl's bedroom. Either copy this design exactly, or adapt the idea to suit

Ribbon Mirror

yourself. The best way to design your own is to fold some real ribbon around the frame, then lay a piece of glass on it to allow you to trace the outline. Notice how the light hits it, creating shadows next to the folds, and highlights where the ribbon catches the light. Try to reproduce this effect using different colors – the technique is the same regardless.

YOU WILL NEED

Wooden mirror frame

Latex (emulsion) paint: violet

Stencil: ribbon (half with shape, half with dot pattern)

Acrylic paint: permanent rose, titanium white, Turner's yellow, aqua green, Payne's gray

Matte medium

Brushes: small household paint-brush; small and medium stencil brushes; fine artist's brush; liner; varnishing brush

Semi-matte water-based varnish

Hint

If you prefer, the shading and highlighting in step 6 can be done with the ribbon-shape stencil in place, using both a stencil brush and a fine artist's brush and just brushing the edges softly with one or the other of them.

1 Paint the wooden mirror frame with two coats of violet latex (emulsion), using a household paintbrush. When the latex (emulsion) is dry, position the ribbon-shape stencil (the portion of the stencil that does not have any dots) on one side of the painted mirror frame. Mix permanent rose and titanium white acrylic together to make a medium pink shade, and stencil half the ribbon in this, using a medium stencil brush.

2 Now turn the stencil around, so that what was previously the top left corner of the ribbon is now the bottom right corner. Stencil the remainder of the ribbon in the same way as for the first half. If the medium pink shade does not completely cover the violet base coat, you will need to apply a second coat of acrylic once the first coat is dry.

3 Before the paint is dry, remove the stencil. Using an artist's brush and permanent rose acrylic (not mixed with white this time), fill in the gaps left by the bridges on the stencil.

4 When the permanent rose is dry, position the ribbon-pattern stencil over the stenciled ribbon so it aligns exactly. Stencil the edges in permanent rose, using a small stencil brush.

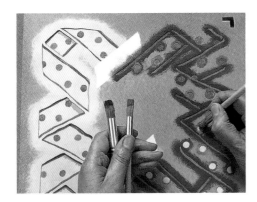

5 Stencil the dots, in permanent rose, Turner's yellow, and aqua green, using small stenciling brushes. Turn the stencil around and repeat steps 4–5. Now lift off the stencil.

6 Add a little Payne's gray and matte medium to the permanent rose for shadows, and white to the medium pink for highlights. Use the artist's brush for this and to fill in the bridges in permanent rose.

7 Mix matte medium with Payne's gray. Using a liner brush, carefully hand-paint a fine deep violet shadow line along the inner and outer edges of the ribbon, parallel to the edges of the mirror frame. This not only adds realism but also helps to define the folded edge of the ribbon.

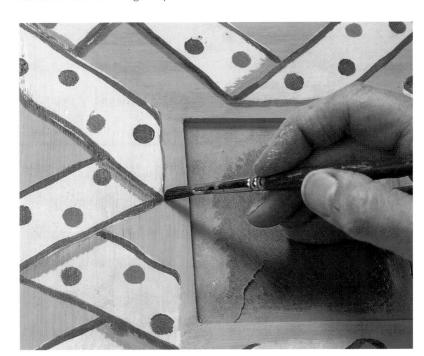

8 Add any further highlights and shadows that are needed to create a realistic, three-dimensional effect. When completely dry, apply two coats of varnish, allowing it to dry between coats.

Inspired by a Venetian marble floor, this design incorporates more modern colors. Bluish mauve, pink, and yellow-orange have been used here, but other colors could be used instead, provided that one is warm and light, another is cool and light,

3-D Floor

and the third is dark. A strong optical illusion is created by the arrangement of three chevrons of the same size but in three colors, an effect similar to the Tumbling Blocks pattern beloved of patchwork enthusiasts.

Stencil two colors, using latex (emulsion) paint only. The background yellow must be painted first. Make marks on the stencil card to help with centering.

YOU WILL NEED

Floor suitable for painting

Tape measure, pencil, straightedge, masking tape

Latex (emulsion) paint: yellow, bluish mauve, pink

Stencil: 2 chevron arms (see design on p49)

Brushes: large household paintbrush; large stencil brush; varnishing brush

Water-based floor varnish

Hints

First measure the floor. Plan the exact size of the repeat motif that will fit into the space, allowing for a border. The border should be about the same width as the thickness of one arm of a chevron. Use a ruler and set square to position and size the rug. Rows should, ideally, start and end with mauve chevrons; try to allow for this when deciding on dimensions.

If desired, deepen the mauve latex (emulsion) with a little black and ultramarine acrylic.

1 Paint the primed floor with two coats of yellow. When dry, mask the border. Place the mauve stencil with one end of the chevron against it. Stencil in mauve.

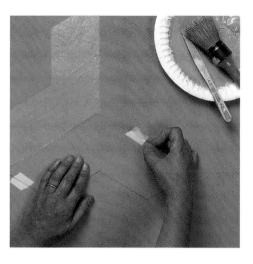

2 Remove the stencil. Place a cut-out portion from one of the stencils against the stenciled chevron, so that it is like a mirror image. Tape it in place.

3 For the next chevron, position the stencil with one end against the border and the other end even with the bottom of the cut-out. Stencil in mauve.

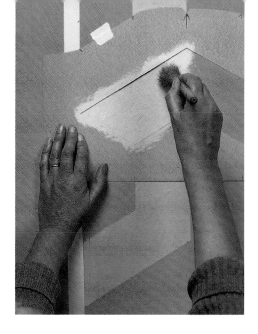

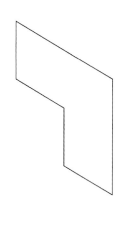

4 Remove the stencil, and then repeat steps 1–3 to complete the row of mauve chevrons alongside the masked edge. By now, the first stenciled motifs should be dry, so you can stencil the pink chevrons between the mauve ones. Position the pink stencil between the first two stenciled mauve chevrons. The edges of the chevron shape in the stencil should align with the edges of the stenciled mauve chevrons. Stencil the chevron in pink. Remove the stencil and repeat for the remaining pink chevrons in the first row. The yellow chevrons are not stenciled, as they are the background color that has already been painted.

5 For each remaining row, place a cut-out portion over what will become the yellow chevron, so that it is back-to-back with a mauve and a pink chevron. Now position the mauve stencil so that the end of the chevron is against the top inner edge of the cut-out and the adjacent, inner edge is against the end of the pink chevron. Stencil in mauve. Remove the stencil, and repeat this step for the remaining mauve chevrons in the row.

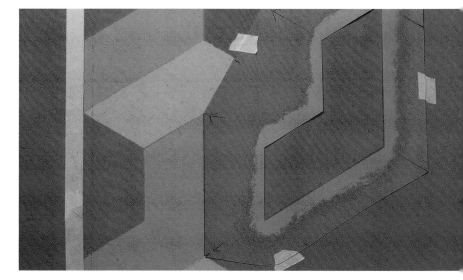

6 For the pink chevrons, place the cut-out over the adjacent yellow chevron, the pink stencil between it, with the mauve chevrons above and below. Stencil in pink. When dry, apply three coats of varnish.

Hints

You will need to cut two identical chevron stencils for this. Save the cut-out portions to help in positioning your design. On the edges of the stencils, mark the corners or borders of the adjacent shapes (these can be seen in the step-by-step photos). When positioning the first stencil, make sure that one long edge of the chevron is parallel to the margin that is covered with masking tape.

Simple Mural

The inspiration for this mural came from an early American primitive painting. The landscape creates a sense of space, while the highlights on the stenciled fence, which is otherwise in shadow, give the impression of light flooding into the room.

YOU WILL NEED

Wall painted with white latex (emulsion)

Latex (emulsion): deep blue, white

Charcoal; plumb line

Stencils: pole, fence (see step 5), small rectangle, ball, highlights, shadows, tufts of grass

Acrylic paint: Hooker's green, Naples yellow, raw sienna, prism violet, Payne's gray, raw umber

Brushes: large household paintbrush; small and large stencil brushes; fine artist's brush

Matte medium

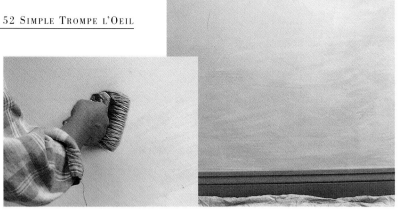

1 Working on a white latex (emulsion)-covered wall, first paint the sky. Using a large, soft, household paintbrush, start at the top with the deepest blue latex (emulsion), thinned with a little water. As you move down the wall, add more and more white to lighten the color. Move the brush swiftly in every direction, smoothing out the paint, so one tone folds into another seamlessly. Carry on down to the baseboard (skirting board).

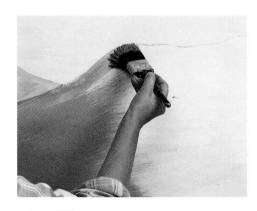

Hints

Adjust the size and spacing of the fence sections, so they fit evenly on the wall. To ensure the poles are vertical, use a plumb line. Coat the string with chalk and attach the top of it to the wall, near the ceiling. Hold the weight against the wall and "twang" the string, leaving a vertical chalk line on the wall. Go over it with pencil.

2 Using charcoal, lightly draw the hills. Mix Hooker's green, Naples yellow, and raw sienna acrylic with white latex (emulsion). Paint the hills in this soft green, adding more yellow and raw sienna now and then to vary the color. Apply it in the same light way as the sky, scuffing the paint and moving one color into another. Paint the distant hills a soft gray-mauve by adding prism violet to the above colors. Keep the paint thin with a splash of water. Paint to the baseboard.

3 Add the clouds with a large, soft stencil brush, blending the paint to make fluffy shapes. Mix a hint of raw sienna into white latex (emulsion). For the underside of the clouds, add a tiny bit of violet and Payne's gray. Keep the clouds well spaced.

4 To start painting the fence, begin with the first pole. Lightly pencil a vertical line using a plumb line (see Hints). Align the pole stencil with this, with the bottom touching the baseboard. Mix enough raw sienna, violet, and white to go around the room – about a jarful should be sufficient. Stencil on the paint using a large, soft stencil brush.

5 Position the fence stencil 1⅜in (3.5cm) from the pole, with the stencil card's bottom resting on the baseboard. The surround must be cut square and to the correct depth. Fill in with the same color.

6 With the small rectangular stencil, fill in the gap in the middle of the fence where the stencil bridge was. This will be less noticeable if done while the previous stenciling is still a little wet.

7 Move the fence stencil along to the next position, placing the left-hand vertical rail on top of the previously stenciled right-hand vertical rail. Stencil as before. Now that two fence sections have been stenciled, it's time to make another fence pole. Position it as in step 4, and stencil as before. Complete the rest of the fence in the same sequence, with a pole between every two fence sections. However, before you proceed any further, you need to follow the next step.

8 While the just stenciled paint is still a little damp, use the small rectangular stencil to extend the top and bottom horizontal rails between the fence sections and pole. Do this as you complete each pole and the adjacent fence sections.

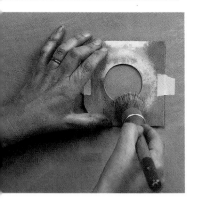

9 Mark the center of the post, match it with the center of the ball, and stencil in the same color as used for the rest of the fence. The previous stenciling does not have to be damp when you do this.

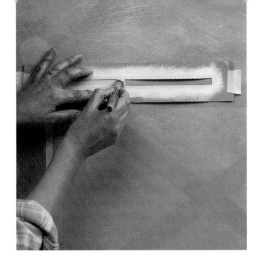

10 Highlight the right side of each vertical rail and pole, and the top of each horizontal rail, by butting the inner edge of the highlights stencil up to it. Stencil in a mix of white and raw sienna, using a small stencil brush.

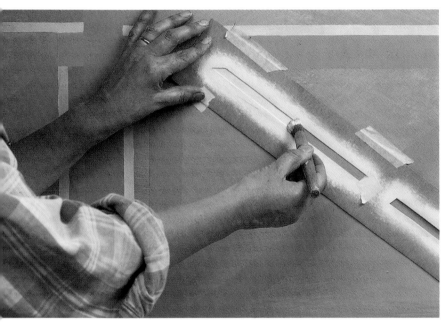

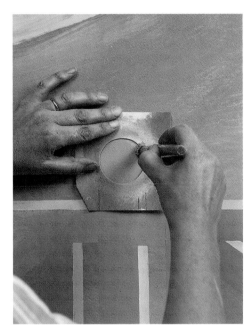

11 As well as highlighting all the horizontal rails and all the vertical rails and poles, highlight the tops of diagonal rails that slope from top left to bottom right.

12 Put the ball stencil back on each stenciled ball, and highlight the right-hand edge with a crescent of the same mixture as used for highlighting earlier.

13 With the ball stencil still in place, mix Payne's gray and raw umber with matte medium, and use this to stencil a very soft shadow on the left edge of the ball, using a small stencil brush.

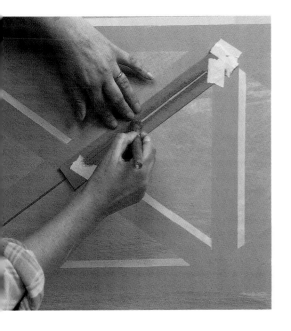

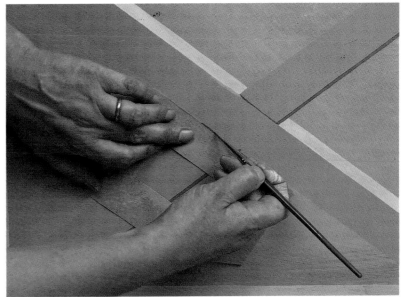

14 Use the shadows stencil and the same mixture as in step 13 to stencil a shadow along the lower edge of each diagonal rail that runs from lower left to top right.

15 With a fine artist's brush and the same mixture that you used for shading in steps 13–14, hand-paint the lines representing joints between rails.

Style Ideas

The mural in this project has deliberately been kept simple, but you could add as much detail to it as you wish. Remember to make anything you add to the distance small, soft, and hazy, and anything in the foreground large and sharp. Or keep the landscape quite bare, and simply add a little butterfly on the fence or some distant birds flying in the sky.

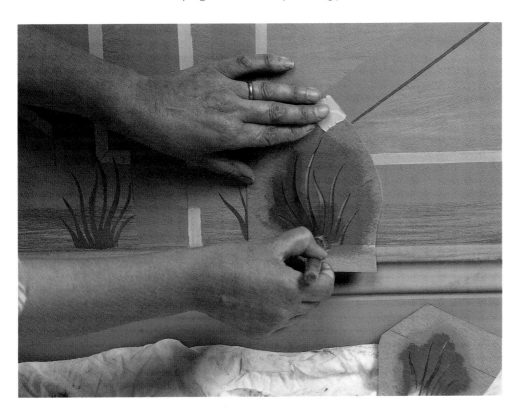

16 With the grass stencil, and a small stencil brush, stencil tufts of grass along the bottom in a mix of Hooker's green and Naples yellow, varying the proportions.

You have to look twice to see that this pretty French plate is not ceramic but is in fact painted straight onto the wall. Copied from an antique Provençal plate (pictured below), it is decorated with graceful flowers in clear colors. The original

French Plate

china plate has a tin and lead glaze, which gives it an attractive, soft blue cast. This effect is mimicked by the blue-gray glaze on the trompe l'oeil plate that is painted on the wall. The plate is stylish on its own, or you could paint a whole set, if you wish.

YOU WILL NEED

Stencils: outer plate, inner plate, flowers

Acrylic paint: titanium white, Payne's gray, alizarin crimson, permanent rose, unbleached titanium, Hooker's green, ultramarine, Naples yellow

Brushes: small, medium and large stencil brushes; fine artist's brush

Matte medium

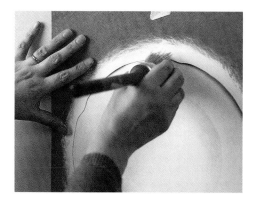

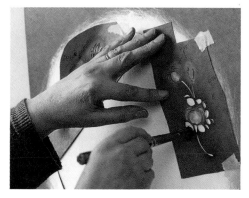

1 With the outer plate stencil, paint the plate white. Leave to dry. With the inner stencil, stipple a soft shadow of Payne's gray diluted with medium and water.

2 Position the flower stencils and stencil them with a small, soft stencil brush. Use a mix of alizarin crimson, rose, and unbleached titanium for the flowers.

3 For the foliage, use a mixture of Hooker's green, unbleached titanium, and a little ultramarine. The stenciling should be done very softly, with the center of each flower the lightest in color. Use separate brushes for the two colors.

4 With a fine artist's brush, hand-paint over the stenciled decoration using slightly darker mixtures of the same colors. Concentrate the darker colors on the outer edges of the flowers. Add stems and lines around the leaves.

Style Ideas

The plate in this project appears to be sitting on a mantelpiece, but you could paint a whole set hanging on a wall, or several plates lined up on a shelf. Look through books about antique ceramics for patterns, or even china advertisements in magazines. Different patterns of blue-and-white china, for example, would look lovely together.

5 Stencil some yellow flower centers with a small brush. Hand-paint circles around a few tiny yellow flowers at the center, in a mix of ultramarine, Payne's gray, and unbleached titanium, using a fine artist's brush.

6 When dry, mix a thin, translucent white glaze from white acrylic and medium. Using a large, soft stencil brush, paint it over the whole plate, to help produce a faded, antique look.

7 With the dark pink mixture from step 4 and a fine artist's brush, paint the narrow edging around the outside of the plate, varying the color a little. It's all right for the line to be a little wobbly.

8 When dry, mix a thin, pale blue-gray glaze from Payne's gray, a little ultramarine, and medium. Paint it over the plate using a medium stencil brush, varying it slightly so that it is not too even.

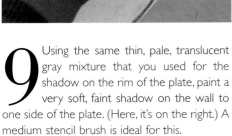

9 Using the same thin, pale, translucent gray mixture that you used for the shadow on the rim of the plate, paint a very soft, faint shadow on the wall to one side of the plate. (Here, it's on the right.) A medium stencil brush is ideal for this.

10 Using a fine artist's brush, hand-paint thin white highlights on the plate, particularly around the rim (just inside the pink edging) on the side opposite to the side casting the shadow on the wall.

Imagine an Aubusson carpet or a native-American "Dazzler" rug on your floor. Painting your own dream carpet is just a matter of copying the colors and the design from the original, although obviously bold, geometric weaves will be

Kilim Rug

easier to reproduce than intricate knotted carpets. This project is a simple kilim, which creates a realistic rug effect due to the subtle variations in the three main colors that are used to make it. If you would like a longer or wider rug, you could simply apply more diamonds within the border. Stenciled floors are surprisingly hard-wearing, provided you apply at least three coats of a good floor varnish.

YOU WILL NEED

Latex (emulsion) paint: white

Tape measure, straightedge, pencil, masking tape

Stencils: 8-pointed star, stepped motif, small square, small circle, double-arrow motif

Acrylic paint: raw sienna, raw umber, alizarin crimson, titanium white, cobalt, Hooker's green, Naples yellow, burnt umber

Brushes: small, medium and large household paint-brushes; small, medium and large stencil brushes; varnishing brush

Floor varnish

1 With a large household paintbrush, apply two coats of primer, then two coats of latex (emulsion), the last tinted with streaks of raw sienna and raw umber. The brush strokes should follow the grain.

2 With a tape measure, straightedge and pencil, mark the border stripes and the diamond shapes. Run masking tape outside the diamonds and outside the wide central stripe of the border.

3 Mix a red shade from alizarin crimson, titanium white, and raw umber. With a medium household paintbrush, paint the red border and the red diamonds. Vary the color a little as you work, with slightly different proportions of the paints. When the paint is dry, carefully remove the masking tape.

4 Using the medium household paintbrush, stencil the stars in red, varying the color slightly. Turn the stencil around so the stars are not too even.

Hints

For the diamonds to be square, the length inside the border must equal the width inside the border multiplied by the number of diamonds. Measure and mark that width along the length, dividing the rug into squares. Mark the center point of each square along both long sides. Now draw a line lengthwise down the exact center of the rug.

With a straightedge, draw a line between the center point of one square on one long side and the point where the edge of the square intersects the lengthwise center line. Repeat for where it intersects the lengthwise center line on the other side of the square. Now repeat for both lines on the other long side. Repeat the process for the other diamonds.

5 Mask outside the narrow stripes. With a small brush, paint these blue using a mixture of cobalt, titanium white, and raw umber, varying the shade.

6 When the stripes are dry, remove the tape. Make sure the red diamonds are completely dry, too, then stencil a blue stepped motif at the center of each red diamond, using a large stencil brush. Once again, vary the blue a little as you work over the whole rug, to add interest and prevent it from looking too flat. From the cut-out portion of the star stencil, cut a small square.

7 Mix a green shade from Hooker's green and Naples yellow. When the stars are dry, stencil a small square at the center of each, in green or blue.

8 When the border is dry, stencil green circles at regular intervals along the red stripe, using the small stencil brush. Change the green from circle to circle, incorporating more blue in some, and more yellow in others, at random.

9 Make sure that the blue stepped motifs at the center of each red diamond are dry. The cut-out portion of the stencil that was used for these can be used to make the stencil for the double-arrow motif, as it is useful for accurate positioning. Cut the double-arrow motif from the center of it, and then position this new stencil exactly over a blue stepped motif. Using the medium stencil brush, stencil it in burnt umber. Repeat for each blue motif, with the arrows all pointing in the same direction. Now stencil a double-arrow motif at each corner of every diamond, still all pointing in the same way. When the whole floor is dry, apply three coats of a good floor varnish, allowing it to dry thoroughly between coats.

Hints

So that the edges of the rug are parallel to the walls, use a tape measure or ruler to make sure each outer edge is the same distance from the nearest wall along its length. The floorboards can also be used as a guide in one direction.

Don't worry about the floorboards showing through. It's part of the fun of trompe l'oeil.

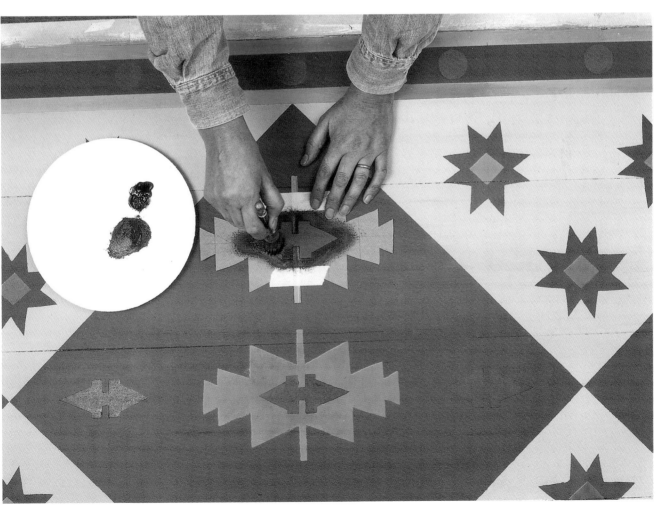

Dull old bathroom cabinets are ripe for the

trompe l'oeil treatment, and what better way to

jazz one up than with a mock window revealing

Bathroom
Cabinet

assorted colorful perfume bottles? This project is a

type of still life and needs to be treated

in a painterly way. It is excellent

practice for still-life painting

techniques and for depicting glass, all

of which will adapt well to other

projects. Stencils are used to give the

perfume bottles crisp outlines, then

they are finished with hand-painting.

YOU WILL NEED
Bathroom cabinet

Masking tape, tracing paper, pencil

Latex (emulsion) paint: mid-brown, dark brown

Stencils: bottles, shelf edge

Acrylic paint: cobalt, titanium white, aqua green, prism violet, black, alizarin crimson, ultramarine, unbleached titanium, light hansa yellow

Brushes: small household paint-brush; small and medium stencil brushes; No. 1, 2, and 9 artist's brushes; varnishing brush

Water-based varnish

1 Mask the edge of the panel with tape, then paint the panel mid-brown, using a small household paintbrush. When the paint is completely dry, transfer the whole design to the painted panel, using tracing paper and a pencil. You can vary the shapes of the bottles as much as you wish, to suit the shape of your own cabinet; the techniques are much the same regardless of the shape.

2 Using the No. 9 brush, paint a dark brown background behind the bottles, around the corners, and along the bottom edge of the panel, leaving the center pale. The paint need not be even: the still life will look more painterly if it is not.

Hints

Save the cut-out shapes from the stencils in this project. They can be cut up and used to make label stencils, and to mask portions of the bottles when stenciling stoppers, liquids, etc. You can also use the cut-out pieces to experiment with different arrangements of bottles to see what will look best on your own cupboard.

3 Mix a pale blue from white with a tiny bit of cobalt and aqua green. With the medium brush, stencil the left-hand bottle, so brown doesn't show through.

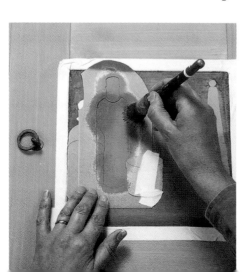

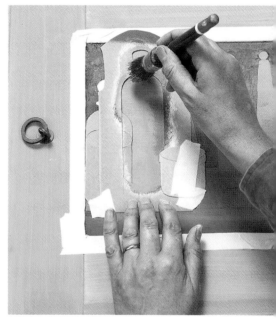

4 Replace the stencil with the one for the next bottle, masking the first bottle with the cut-out portion. Stencil in a pale blue mix of cobalt, violet, and white.

5 Add a little black to the pale blue mixture from step 4, and, using the same (medium) stencil brush, darken the edges a little with this. The left edge should be slightly darker than the right edge.

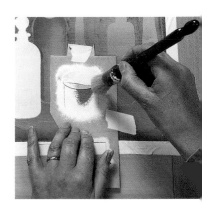

6 Place the cut-out portion of the bottle top from the stencil over the top of the bottle to mask it. With a medium stencil brush, stencil the stopper in black. Remove the stencil and cut-out portion.

7 Put the stencil for the pink jar in place, masking the lid with the cut-out portion from the stencil. Using a medium stencil brush, stencil in the jar with a mixture of a tiny bit of alizarin crimson in white paint.

8 Mask the jar with the cut-out portion, and the top of the lid with the cut-out of the nail polish bottle. Stencil the lid in a mixture of aqua green and white.

9 Add the lid cut-out so that everything but the rim is masked. Stencil the rim in a darker mix of aqua green and white. Now remove the stencil and cut-outs.

10 As in steps 4–5, stencil the nail polish bottle in crimson with a black stopper; the dark blue bottle in a mixture of black, ultramarine, and unbleached titanium, under a mid-brown cork; and the right-hand bottle in two bluish mauve shades of cobalt, and violet mixed with white. Darken the colors for the shadows, but keep the effect soft.

11 Using a small stencil brush and the shelf-edge stencil, paint the edge of the glass shelf in a mixture of aqua green and white, adding more white for the middle, and a little black when you stencil the edges. Then remove the stencil.

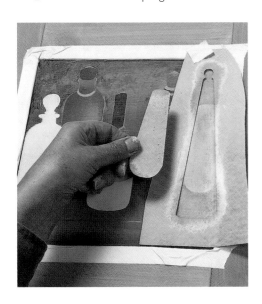

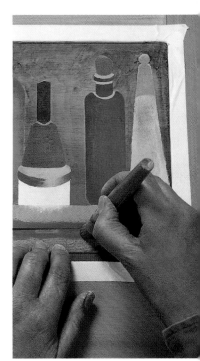

Style Ideas

With their interesting shapes, perfume bottles make an ideal trompe l'oeil design for a bathroom. The idea will also work well with other subjects, such as jars of preserves, condiments, herbs, and spices on a kitchen shelf; china in a dining room cabinet; books, pencils, and the like in a study; or toys in a wardrobe in a child's bedroom.

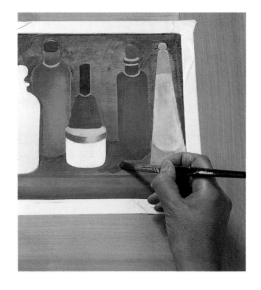

12 With the No. 9 brush and a thin mixture of aqua green, black, and a little white, hand-paint the top of the glass shelf, around the jar and bottles. Paint it quite roughly and thinly so that the brown shows through.

13 With a darker shade of the ultramarine mix from step 10, hand-paint the shadows on the shoulders of the dark blue bottle, using the No. 2 artist's brush. There should be more shadows on the left.

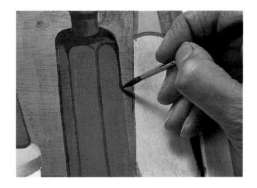

14 Use the same color and brush to paint lines down the faceted edges and fill in the bottom of the bottle. Dilute this mixture and outline the adjacent bottle.

15 Replace the left-hand stencil. Mask the top of it with part of the cut-out. Mix yellow and aqua green with water. Stencil the liquid, varying the proportions a little.

16 With the stencil and cut-out still in place, also mask the bottom of the bottle with more of the cut-out. Add extra aqua green to the mixture from step 15 and, using the same (medium) brush, stencil the surface of the liquid, making the edges darkest.

17 Mix together unbleached titanium, white, and a tiny bit of crimson. With a rectangular stencil and a medium stencil brush, stencil the label on the pink jar.

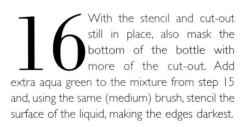

18 With the No. 2 brush, add lettering. Mix white and violet for the mauve bottle, and use diluted black for the rest.

19 Stencil soft shadows: diluted black on the jar; and a thin mix of violet, unbleached titanium, and black on the mauve bottle.

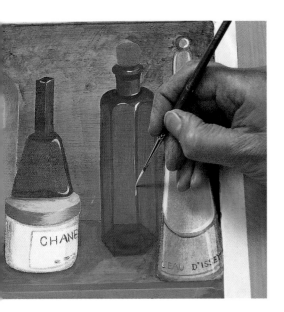

20 Using a No. 1 brush, add white flecks and streaks to highlight the bottles and jar, especially on the right sides.

21 Add highlights to bring out the "not to be taken" raised lettering painted in thinned black on the blue bottle.

22 Still using the No. 1 brush, add violet and pale blue highlights and decoration to the second bottle from the left, and black specks to the cork in the blue bottle. When dry, create the impression of glass by lightly scuffing streaks of white diagonally across it with a small household paintbrush, keeping paint dry. When the paint is dry, remove the tape; apply varnish.

Here's a box in which a small cowboy or cowgirl can keep their treasures.

Texan Chest

YOU WILL NEED
Wooden box

Latex (emulsion) paint: teal (or other color), white

Pencil, straightedge

Stencils: stripes, horse and rider, cacti, aloe plants

Acrylic paint: raw sienna, burnt sienna, Payne's gray, burnt umber, unbleached titanium, Naples yellow

Brushes: household paintbrush; medium stencil brush; fine and medium artist's brushes; varnishing brush

Matte medium

Semi-matte water-based varnish

A 1950s-print style cowboy gallops across a striped blanket, while sunset-red cacti and aloe plants grow along the side. Nearly all of the decoration is stenciled.

Style Ideas

This box is obviously tailor-made for a young child's bedroom or playroom, but it would also be fun in a 1950s-style family room or at the foot of a bed, for either of which the theme would tie in well. Boxes and chests provide an inviting surface for trompe l'oeil stenciling, and for this project any old chest or trunk could be given a new lease of life.

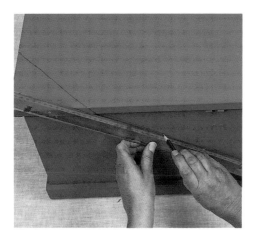

1 Using a household paintbrush, paint the box with latex (emulsion) in teal or the color of your choice. Plan the design so that a rectangular blanket will appear to be thrown diagonally across the top, with the corners hanging down. Using a pencil and a straightedge, draw the blanket on the top, the sides, and the ends.

2 With a household paintbrush, paint the blanket in white latex (emulsion) with a little raw sienna acrylic mixed into it. Brush the paint on roughly so that the blanket will look coarsely woven. In order to cover the base coat completely, you will probably need to apply a second coat after the first has dried, particularly if the base coat is dark.

3 It is easiest to paint the box lid first, and then paint the corners of the blanket that appear to hang down over the sides and ends. Don't forget to paint the edges, too – you will need to use a medium artist's brush for this, rather than the household brush that you used in steps 1–2.

4 When the white background is dry, position the stripes stencil diagonally across one corner of the lid, parallel to the edge of the blanket. Using a medium stencil brush, stencil the stripes in burnt sienna, stenciling over the edge of the lid, too. Repeat on the diagonally opposite corner.

5 Place the stripes stencil on the corner of the blanket that is on the front of the box, aligning it with the stripes already stenciled on the lid. Stencil these stripes in the same way.

6 When the stripes are dry, place a stripes stencil across one of the remaining corners of the lid. Stencil in a mixture of Payne's gray, burnt umber, and unbleached titanium. Repeat for the last corner.

7 Position the horse stencil on the blanket so that it will be in the center when the rider is added. Mix raw sienna, Naples yellow, and unbleached titanium together to produce a soft mustard shade. Using a medium stencil brush, stencil the horse with this color. Remove the stencil.

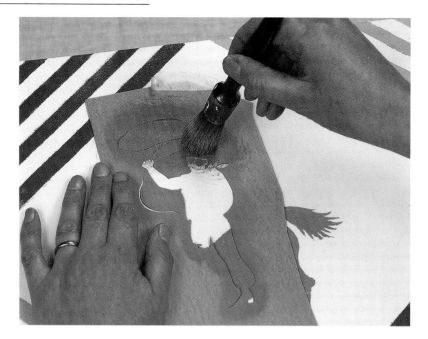

8 When the horse is dry, place the cowboy stencil on top of it. Mix the same colors as in step 7 into a more browny mustard shade this time, and stencil the cowboy with it, once again using a medium stencil brush. Remove the stencil and fill in the gaps left by the stencil bridges.

9 Now stencil cacti and aloe plants around the sides and ends of the box, using burnt sienna and a medium stencil brush.

Hints

Repeat patterns such as stripes and checks are much easier and quicker to stencil than to paint by hand. While most of the other stripes in this book have been stenciled singly, here multiple stripes are cut from the stencil. The main thing to remember is to try to make the stripes look continuous, by blending the colors together at the ends while they are still damp. Fading the paint away at the ends as you stencil also helps, as it prevents the color from being too dense when the stripe ends overlap.

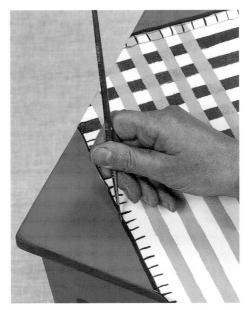

Style Ideas

A trompe l'oeil throw over a box or trunk would look good in a variety of designs. Sticking with the Wild West theme, you could use a Navajo Indian blanket as the basis of your design. Or for a completely different look which still uses the stenciled-stripes technique, you could produce a trompe l'oeil tartan throw. A kilim design would also work well as a painted throw. Or consider other simple embroidery patterns apart from the blanket stitch used here.

10 Use the stripes stencil and a medium stencil brush to add stripes along the bottom of the box, beneath the cacti and aloe plants. Once again, use burnt sienna. Try to make the stripes look continuous, with no obvious juncture showing where the stencil ended. Also paint the edge of the lid, outside the blanket, in burnt sienna to match.

11 The blanket should look as though it has been neatly edged with blanket-stitch embroidery. Using a fine artist's brush, paint thin lines of burnt umber at right angles to the edge of the blanket, joined by a thin line in the same color just along the edge. Paint these mock stitches all the way around the blanket, spacing them equally.

12 Still using the fine brush, paint a very thin line of raw sienna just inside the blanket stitching, to look like the edge of the seam. Hand-paint a saddle on the horse in the same color. Hand-paint a shadow under the horse in Naples yellow. Use burnt sienna to lightly delineate the saddle outline, stirrups, and bridle, and the cowboy's features and clothes. Mix raw umber with matte medium, and paint a faint shadow around the edge of the blanket, to create a relief effect. When completely dry, apply two or three coats of semi-matte varnish.

Small, attractive boxes that will hold CDs, postcards, and other paraphernalia are invaluable around the home and make great presents.

Desk Box

On these boxes a design based on a single shape with a shadow looks startlingly three-dimensional. Whatever the geometric shape, the technique is the same – and couldn't be easier.

YOU WILL NEED

Small wooden box

Latex (emulsion) paint: blue, yellow

Stencils: geometric shape, shadow

Acrylic paint: permanent rose, Payne's gray

Brushes: small household paintbrush; small and medium stencil brushes; liner; varnishing brush

Matte medium

Water-based varnish

1 Using a small household brush, paint the box with latex (emulsion) in blue or the color of your choice. Leave to dry, then apply a second coat. Paint the inside with two coats of a contrasting color of latex (emulsion), such as yellow. When dry, stencil a simple geometric shape such as a circle, oval, diamond, square, rectangle, or triangle all over the outside of the box. Use a medium stencil brush and an acrylic color that contrasts with the box color, such as permanent rose. Leave to dry.

Hints

Shadows are probably the trompe l'oeil artist's most useful device, creating an instant illusion of three-dimensionality at the flick of a paintbrush. But for trompe l'oeil to be effective, it's essential that the shadows are in the correct position. This means that you must always decide from which direction the light will appear to be coming, and place the shadows accordingly. If just one is out of place, it will make the whole design look odd. Be sure to make the shadow the right shape when you are cutting its stencil. And when you are stenciling it, take care to position it right next to the stenciled geometric shape, without a gap.

2 Make up a thin mixture of Payne's gray and matte medium. Place the shadow stencil close to one of the spots, and lightly stencil the shadow with a small, soft brush. Stencil the other shadows in the same way, making sure they are in the same position.

Style Ideas

Stenciling is ideal for this project: the shapes are simplicity itself to cut, and the motifs are repeated so frequently that hand-painting them would be tedious. Also, the crisp outline that stenciling imparts ensures maximum impact. However, don't let the ease of stenciling these shapes encourage you to use too many of them – for the design to look right, generous spacing is important.

3 Using a liner, hand-paint the rim of the box in the same color as you used for the stenciled shapes. It won't be too difficult to avoid wobbling, so masking the edges should not be necessary. Leave to dry completely, then apply two coats of varnish, allowing the varnish to dry between coats.

This painted roller blind looks as though a fine, translucent, Indian printed shawl has been hung over it.

Indian Print Blind

The pattern has been kept simple and light, with just a hint of shadow to lift it from a plain background. The delicate nature of the pattern makes this blind suitable for the kitchen, bedroom, or bathroom, especially with country or colonial-style furniture and accessories.

YOU WILL NEED
Roller blind

Masking tape

Ruler

Stencils: border line, repeated flowers, leaf border

Acrylic paint: chromium oxide green, aqua green, titanium white, permanent rose, raw umber

Brushes: household brush; small, medium and large stencil brushes; ¼in (6mm) liner

Matte medium

Style Ideas

The traditional pattern and sun-drenched colors of this blind are typical of Indian designs. Find inspiration for new projects in examples from other countries; stencils have been used all over the world since the Middle Ages in homes and at sacred sites, in a wonderful variety of patterns and colors.

1 Mask off a 5in (12cm)-deep rectangle at the bottom of the blind, about 2in (5cm) from the edges. Use a household brush to fill the rectangle with a soft green mixed from chromium oxide green, aqua green, and white. When dry, remove the tape.

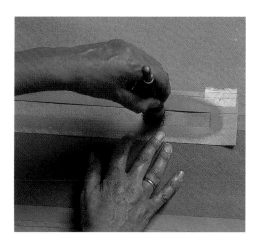

2 Mix a pink color from permanent rose, raw umber, and titanium white. Use the border-line stencil and a medium stencil brush to apply a ¾in (2cm)-wide pink border outside the green rectangle. Continue the pink border up both sides of the blind.

3 Center the repeated-flowers stencil above the green rectangle. Using a small stencil brush, paint the leaves and stems with the green color from step 1, allowing it to fade up the stem.

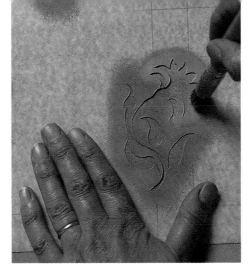

4 Using the pink color and the small stencil brush, paint the petals of each flower, working inward toward the center from the outside of the flower and leaving some of the roller blind showing at the center of each flower.

5 Repeat steps 3–4 over the rest of the roller blind. Mix an off-white color using white and a little raw umber. Center the leaf-border stencil over the green rectangle at the bottom of the blind, and use a large stencil brush to apply the off-white color. Repeat the process across the remainder of the bottom of the roller blind. Allow time for the paint to dry thoroughly before moving on to the next step.

6 To make a thin, soft-white glaze, mix some matte medium with the off-white color from step 5, and then add enough water to make it the consistency of very thin cream. Use a household brush to apply the glaze, brushing in one direction only, all over the roller blind between the pink borders. Mask around the borders if you wish, but do not worry about evenness. This effect will make the "hanging" look soft and fabric-like.

7 To finish the blind, mix a glaze as directed in step 6, but this time add enough raw umber to produce a soft brown color. Using a ¼in (6mm) liner, paint the glaze along the outside edges of the pink borders. Don't attempt to make the lines absolutely straight and even by using a ruler; a slightly wobbly edge will look softer and more realistic than a perfectly straight one. Painting a narrower line at one side than at the other side, and at the bottom, will also add to the realism. This subtle shadow effect will make the "hanging" appear to stand out from the rest of the roller blind, adding to the illusion.

The inspiration behind a curtain to be painted and stenciled on a wall comes from a naïvely painted wall in a 12th-century Catalonian chapel

Stenciled Curtain

in the Spanish Pyrénées. Trompe l'oeil hangings, like the one under the hall window on the right, were often painted on walls in Italy during the Renaissance of the 14th century. The curtain can be applied to any fairly flat vertical surface and makes a striking feature in any room. Its formal decorative quality makes it best suited to a main bedroom, living room, or entrance hall.

YOU WILL NEED

Plumb line

Stencils: scallop border, diamond border, small cross, diamond stripes, small diamond, cross motif, medium diamond, cloverleaf

Acrylic paint: Naples yellow, red oxide, chromium oxide green, cerulean blue, raw umber, titanium white, alizarin crimson, Payne's gray

Brushes: small, medium and large stencil brushes; thin liner; household paintbrushes

Pencil

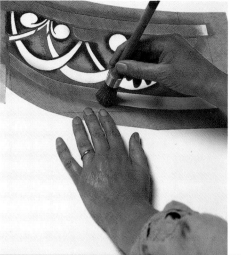

1 Divide the chosen area of wall into sections to work out how many scallop border and diamond repeats will fit into the space. (Each scallop is the width of two diamonds.) Start by painting the top border of the curtain, using the scallop border stencil. Mix a strong yellow from Naples yellow and red oxide, diluted with a little water. Using the medium stencil brush, paint the edges of the scallop border with this yellow color. Also paint the semicircular motifs along the top of the stencil in the same color. You may need to mask adjacent areas with card as you work, as the motifs are quite close together in this stencil.

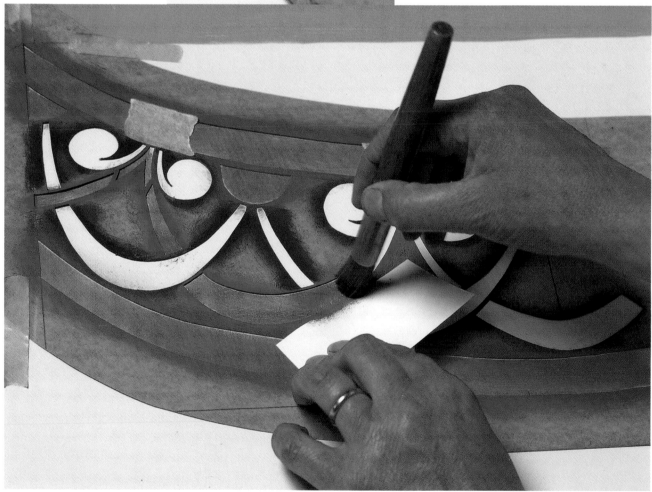

2 Mix a green from chromium oxide green, cerulean blue, and a little raw umber and titanium white. Mix a red from alizarin crimson and a little raw umber, white, and red oxide. Use a medium stencil brush to paint the green and red portions, masking with card as necessary.

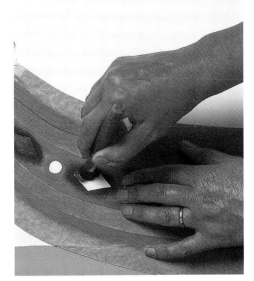

3 Remove the stencil and use a liner and the yellow, green, and red to fill in the gaps left by the stencil bridges. Turn over the stencil, when it is dry, to paint the adjacent portions of the border in reverse.

4 Use the same three colors, a large and a small stencil brush, and the diamond border stencil to paint the scallop edging at the bottom of the curtain, leaving the right corner unpainted for the curled edge.

5 Use a pencil to sketch in the curled bottom of the curtain, or trace the shape (best seen in the step 7 photograph) and adjust it to the correct size.

Hint

When planning the position of the curtain design on the wall, sketch a rough outline first on a piece of paper. This rough draft will help to ensure that the scallop borders and overall diamond pattern which you have created fit into the area exactly. It will also help you to work out the amount of materials you are likely to need for this decoration.

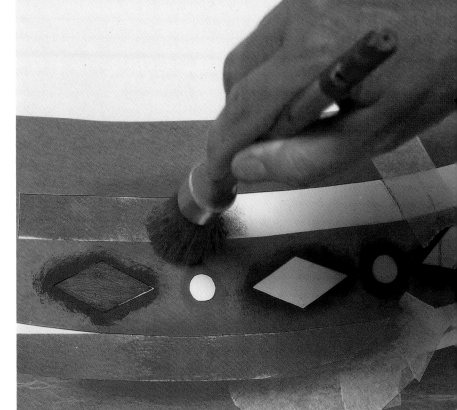

6 Replace the stencil so that it overlaps a painted section, curving it upward slightly to meet the hand-drawn lines. Mask it as shown. Stencil the yellow, green, and red sections as before.

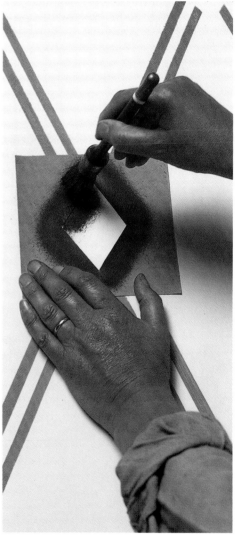

7 Remove the stencil and tape. Paint the yellow portions on the underside of the curled-up corner by hand, using the thin liner. Pencil in the complete diamond, partial diamond, and circle motifs on this curled-up bottom corner; use the diamond border stencil as a guide. Paint these with the thin liner brush by hand, using the same red and green mixtures as for the rest of the border. With the small cross stencil and the small stencil brush, paint red crosses on the underside edge of the curled-up side. (These can be seen in the photo accompanying step 14.)

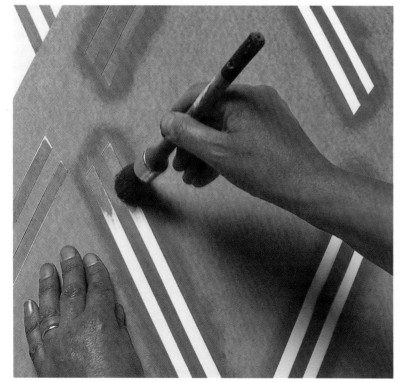

8 Position the diamond-stripes stencil centrally beneath the top border. With the medium stencil brush, stencil yellow diamond stripes. Reposition the stencil using the painted stripes as a guide. Continue until the whole area is covered.

9 When dry, use the small diamond stencil and the medium stencil brush to paint red diamonds where the yellow stripes meet. As you work down the wall, vary the shade of red by adding more raw umber or more white.

10 With the cross-motif stencil and the medium stencil brush, use the same mixtures as previously to stencil a green and red pattern in the center of each diamond formed by the yellow stripes. Repeat the procedure across the curtain, once again varying the shades a little as you work.

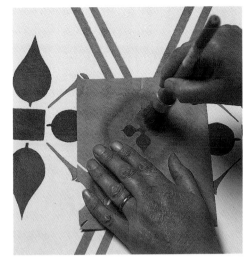

11 Position the medium diamond stencil over a red diamond, and cover the red diamond with the cut-out portion of the small diamond stencil. Using a small stencil brush, paint a green border around each red diamond. When dry, use the cloverleaf stencil to add a yellow cloverleaf to the center.

Hints

If desired, use a plumb line (see Hints, p. 52) and a carpenter's level (spirit level) to lightly pencil a grid on the wall, then mark the points of the diamonds in staggered rows on the grid.

If you vary the shades of red by adding different amounts of raw umber or white paint color to it, be sure to keep mixing and remixing the paint as you work. A good range of shades of red will give the curtain a fine textured effect.

12 Use the small cross stencil and a small stencil brush to add a yellow cross to each red rectangle. Draw a yellow rectangle around it with a liner.

13 Mix a dark brown-gray from raw umber and Payne's gray and hand-paint fine lines along each yellow diamond stripe and around the yellow scallop borders. Steady your hand by resting it on your little finger, but don't worry if your lines wobble; this will add to the range of textures.

14 Thin raw umber with water. Use a small household paintbrush to fill in the wall behind the curled edge of the curtain with the diluted paint. Apply a less diluted mixture along the inside and outside edges of the curl to indicate its shadow.

15 Dilute the raw umber with more water so that it has a very thin consistency. With the household paintbrush, paint the light shadow cast onto the curtain itself by the curled-up corner. The farther the shadow is from the corner, the softer it should be.

Style Ideas

Paneling and walls have been popular subjects in trompe l'oeil for centuries. For inspiration, study the paneling in historic houses to help you understand the play of light and shade in the many types of paneling found there.

16 Dilute some raw umber to the same consistency as in step 14. Still using the household paintbrush, paint above and below the curtain edges to suggest a wood-paneled wall behind the curtain. Fill all the area in, being very careful not to get any paint on the scalloped borders. The brush strokes here are used to create the effect of the woodgrain, and so they should follow the direction of the grain. This means that the raised area (technically known as the muntin) between two side-by-side panels should be painted with vertical brush strokes, as should the vertical strips of "molding" at either side of the muntin. (This can be seen more clearly in the photograph accompanying the next step.) The rest of the paneling should be painted with horizontal brush strokes.

17 With the household paintbrush, create three-dimensional effects in the mock wooden paneling above and below the curtain. Use undiluted raw umber to shade the horizontal moldings; undiluted raw umber mixed with Payne's gray to pick out the vertical molding to the right of the central muntin; and undiluted Payne's gray to highlight the vertical molding to the left of the central muntin. The brush strokes should be vertical for the vertical moldings, and horizontal for the horizontal moldings. (Depicting paneling in this way is a classic trompe l'oeil technique.)

18 With diluted raw umber acrylic and the household paintbrush, hand-paint shadowy drape lines to make the curtain look more like fabric. Keep the lines simple, using a few long, flowing strokes. Use the same paint to add fine lines down the creases of the curtain from the raised edges of the scallop border.

This key cupboard is a small project which is fun to do. Paint the cupboard however you like, as long as it is not in the same colors as the key and label. You can draw around a key and also around a label straight onto the stencil card. If you keep

Key Cupboard

the key and label handy, along with the string, they will prove useful for referring to when you are hand-painting the detailing. Although this project involves decorating a cupboard for a garden shed or garage, you could use the same design indoors, perhaps on a board with hooks where keys could be hung, or on the side of a box in which to store them.

YOU WILL NEED

Latex (emulsion) paint: blue, white, black, green

Stencils: key with label (traced from design on right), circles

Acrylic paint: burnt umber, Payne's gray, burnt sienna, titanium white, cadmium red

Brushes: small and medium stenciling; liner; medium artist's; varnishing; household paintbrush

Matte medium

Water-based varnish

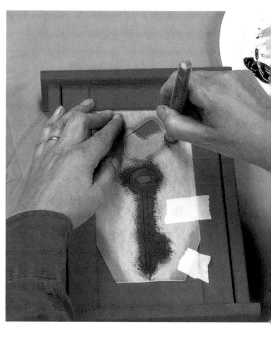

Style Ideas

This idea could be adapted to identify the contents of a variety of cupboards or other storage pieces, such as boxes. The simplicity of the image is part of its charm, so try to think of other bold shapes that would look graphic and fun on a cupboard door or a box. Pruning shears, a terracotta pot, a hammer, or a wrench are possibilities in the garage or shed, while a coffee cup could go on a kitchen cupboard.

1 Paint the cupboard in a blue latex (emulsion) softened with a little white and black. When dry, use a small stencil brush to stencil the key in a mix of burnt umber and Payne's gray, applying two coats.

2 With a medium stencil brush, stencil the label in a mix of burnt sienna, Payne's gray and titanium white. Again, you will need to apply two coats to prevent the base coat from showing through.

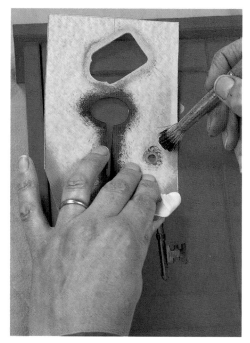

3 Using a liner, paint highlights on the key in a mix of titanium white and a little Payne's gray. Apply them along the shank of the key, to portions of the inner and outer top edges and to part of the locking mechanism at the base of the key.

4 With a small stencil brush and a small circle stencil, stencil the nail from which the key is hanging, using a mix of burnt umber and Payne's gray. In order to look as though the key is hanging on the nail, it should overlap the key a little.

5 With the same mix of burnt umber and Payne's gray used in the previous step, hand-paint a narrow shadow along the edges of the key using a liner.

6 Again using the mixture of burnt umber and Payne's gray, paint a narrow, dark shadow around the lower edge of the label, using the liner. Also paint the hole.

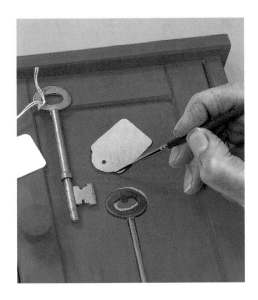

7 With the liner, paint a soft, very subtle shadow of Payne's gray diluted with matte medium around the label, outside the previous shadow.

8 Pencil in some string hanging from the label. The easiest way to do this is to arrange a real label and some string in the desired position and copy them.

9 Mix a little burnt umber with titanium white. Hand-paint over the pencil lines with this color, again using the liner. Make the ends of the string look as though they are slightly frayed.

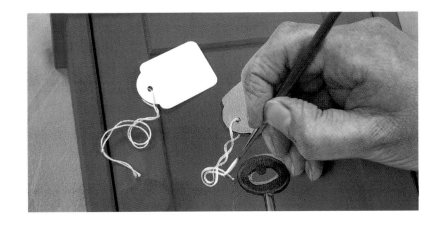

10 Position the medium circle stencil so it overlaps the lower edge of the label, and stencil the thumbtack in red, using the small stencil brush. When dry, stencil a second coat so the blue base coat doesn't show.

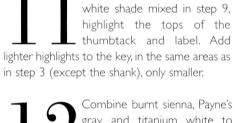

11 Using the liner and the off-white shade mixed in step 9, highlight the tops of the thumbtack and label. Add lighter highlights to the key, in the same areas as in step 3 (except the shank), only smaller.

12 Combine burnt sienna, Payne's gray, and titanium white to make a slightly darker color than you originally used for stenciling the label in step 2. Put the stencil for the key and label back in position, and stencil a little shading around the edges of the label, using a medium stencil brush. Remove the stencil.

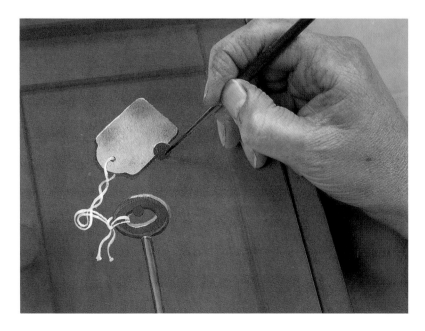

13 Add a little matte medium to Payne's gray, and shade the bottom half of the thumbtack with this, using the liner. Taking care over shading and highlighting even the smallest items will make a great deal of difference to the three-dimensionality of your design, particularly when the items are in a bright color, like this red thumbtack.

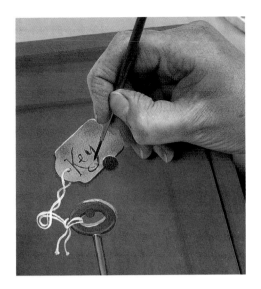

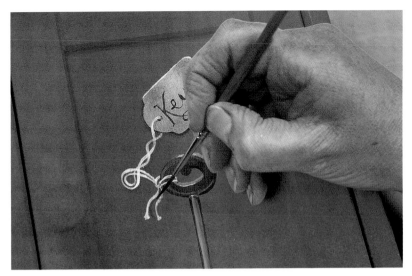

14 When the label is completely dry, pencil the word "Keys" on it. Now use the liner and the mixture of burnt umber and Payne's gray from steps 1 and 6 to hand-paint over the penciled lettering.

15 Using the liner and Payne's gray diluted with matte medium, hand-paint the shadows cast by the string. Note that the shadows in this case are not exactly alongside the string, which adds to the illusion.

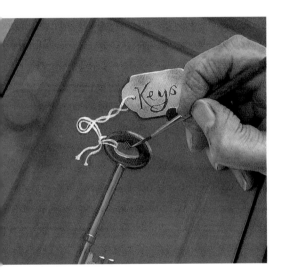

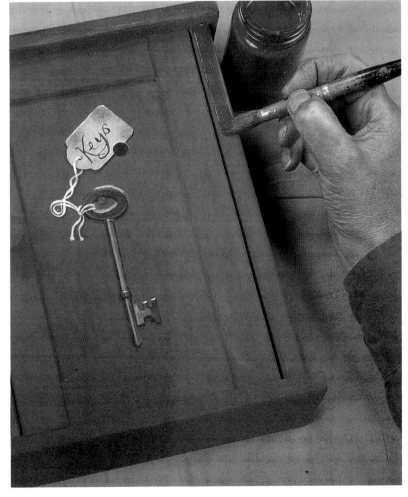

16 With undiluted Payne's gray acrylic and the liner, carefully paint thin parallel lines across the head of the nail from which the key is hanging. Because it is only slightly lighter than the color of the nail, this will produce a realistic textured effect.

17 Finally, paint the edge of the cupboard in green latex (emulsion) softened with a little black and white, using a medium artist's brush. Stencil a green circle on the knob. When dry, apply two coats of varnish.

This design is typical of the mid-Victorian Gothic revival made popular by Pugin and Burges. Strong, opulent colors were *de rigueur*, as well as lots of gold! The stenciled frieze with its shadow creates the impression of a plaster frieze

Gothic Frieze

standing proud on the wall. It works very well beneath either an existing coving or a trompe l'oeil painted molding under a high ceiling. The ideal wall colors are strong yellow, vibrant dark red, or dark green. A nice finishing touch would be trompe l'oeil plates stenciled on the walls beneath the frieze.

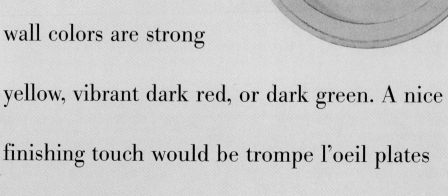

YOU WILL NEED

Wall painted in strong color of latex (emulsion)

Stencils: frieze main design (traced from step 11 photo), frieze shadows (see steps 1–3)

Latex (emulsion) paint: white

Black felt-tip pen, straightedge, pencil, masking tape

Acrylic paint: raw umber

Brushes: small household paint-brush; small and medium stencil brushes; liner

1 You need to make two stencils of the frieze, one for the overall design and one for the shadows. Transfer the design onto stencil card and cut it out very accurately. (A heat pen will make this easier, although it is not essential.) Using the stencil you have just cut out, stencil the design onto a second piece of stencil card with raw umber or another dark paint. The painted, uncut second stencil is shown on the left.

2 When the paint is dry, put the original stencil back on the second one, but to the left and down slightly, as shown above. Stencil the design again, but this time using white paint.

Style Ideas

Trompe l'oeil plates are an ideal accompaniment to this project. Stencil the basic plate as shown on pages 56–59, and add a simple stencil motif such as the flower shown opposite. If your wall is yellow, blue-and-white plates look sensational, but obviously the colors can be chosen to match your decor.

3 The dark, first coat of paint forms the shadows behind the white design on the second stencil, as shown above. Cut out these shadows. You now have one stencil (the original stencil) for the overall design, and a second stencil for the shadows.

4 With a household paintbrush, paint a white band across the top of the wall for the fake molding. Use a black felt-tip pen to draw a cross-section of the molding at one end of the white band. With a straightedge, pencil in appropriate shadow lines.

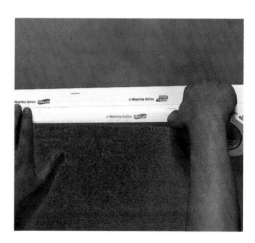

5 With a straightedge, pencil two pairs of parallel lines ¾in (2cm) apart along the length of the white band. These will become shadow lines in the molding. Make the top pair slightly farther apart than the bottom pair.

6 Mask outside both pairs of lines. (Make sure that your tape is narrow enough not to cover up the area that is to be painted between the other pair of lines.)

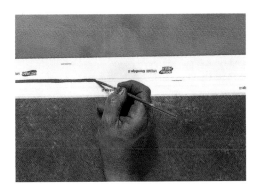

7 Paint these two shadow lines in raw umber across the width of the wall, using a liner. When the paint is dry, very carefully remove the masking tape by pulling it back on itself slowly.

8 Fix your original stencil (the main design, without shadows) below the painted molding. Mark a registration mark on a piece of masking tape through a hole in one corner of the stencil.

9 Using the medium stencil brush, stencil the design in white latex (emulsion), dabbing lightly to avoid smearing it under the stencil (particularly with this stencil's narrow bridges). Leave to dry.

10 Remove the first stencil. Line up the second (shadow) stencil on the registration mark. Stencil the shadows in white mixed with raw umber, using the small brush.

11 Repeat steps 8–10 across the width of the wall beneath the painted molding. As you go, touch up any flaws by hand with a liner, and use a damp cloth to remove any stray bits of paint.

The fig-leaf stencil used on this blue painted basket was cut out after real fig leaves were traced onto stencil card. The stencil for the main veins was then made from the cut-out

Garden Basket

portion. Applications of various subtly different shades of green give the leaves a natural, textured look. The finished stenciling will be quite hard-wearing, but, as your basket ages, it will acquire an attractive antique patina.

YOU WILL NEED
Garden basket

Stencils: butterfly, main fig leaf, fig-leaf veins

Acrylic paint: red oxide, titanium white, burnt sienna, Payne's gray, Turner's yellow, Hooker's green, Naples yellow

Brushes: ½in (12mm) flat artist's brush; ¼in (6mm) liner; small, medium and large stencil brushes; thin liner; long, fine, artist's brush; varnishing brush

Marine varnish

Style Ideas

Nothing beats the variety of the wonderful shapes and forms to be found in nature, so look around you for possible shapes to copy for stencils. Flora and fauna are especially appropriate subjects for a garden project. If you want to use insects, however, those which often alight or perch will look the most realistic. Butterflies, ladybugs (ladybirds), dragonflies, and bumblebees are all possibilities.

1 Use a ½in (12mm) flat artist's brush to hand-paint a red oxide line along the rim of the basket. Paint the rim on all four sides of the basket, and let it dry thoroughly. If the base coat shows through, apply another coat of the red oxide.

2 Position the double-line stencil on the basket handle and paint with red oxide, using a medium stencil brush. Reposition the stencil to paint the remainder of the handle. When dry, repeat with a second coat.

3 When the stripes are dry, position the butterfly stencil on the handle and use a small stencil brush to apply two coats of titanium white, letting the first dry thoroughly before applying the second. Repeat on one inside wall of the basket.

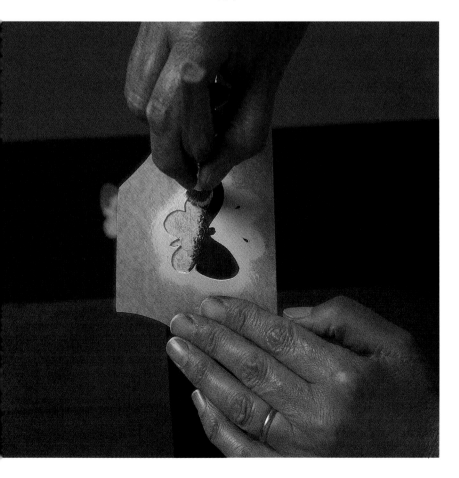

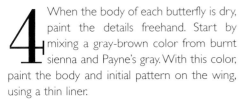

4 When the body of each butterfly is dry, paint the details freehand. Start by mixing a gray-brown color from burnt sienna and Payne's gray. With this color, paint the body and initial pattern on the wing, using a thin liner.

5 Mix an orange shade from Turner's yellow and a little white. Using the liner, paint orange tips on the wings. Add a pattern of dots on the wing tips with Turner's yellow, a pair of antennae with titanium white, and a few patches of the gray-brown.

6 The three overlapping leaves are painted one at a time, using two fig-leaf stencils. Place the solid fig-leaf stencil in the middle of the basket base. Mix a green shade from Hooker's green and Naples yellow, and with a large stencil brush paint the leaf. When the first coat is dry, apply a second coat if necessary in order to cover the base color completely. Leave to dry.

7 Mix a lighter green by adding white and Turner's yellow to your existing mix. Using the large stencil brush, stipple this new shade over the dry painted leaf in places, to add a grainy, uneven texture.

Hints

Many people are wary of freehand painting, but it need not be daunting. Before you begin, practice your chosen design on some scrap paper until you are happy with it. As you grow in confidence, try out different colors and paint mixes as you work. Don't worry if the lines and outlines are not perfect – this is part of the charm of handmade crafts, and suits trompe l'oeil pieces taken from nature particularly well.

8 Take the vein stencil and position it centrally over the painted fig leaf, without removing the main stencil. (Leaving the original stencil in position helps prevent paint accidentally going over the edge when the new design is close to the edge.)

9 Use the lighter green color that you mixed in step 7 and the small stencil brush to stroke on the veins. It does not matter if the lines you paint are broken or uneven; this adds character to the natural effect.

10 Remove both stencils and use a long, fine artist's brush to hand-paint some more veins in the same light green color that you used for the veins in the previous step. These hand-painted veins should be thinner and more delicate than the stenciled veins, tapering to almost nothing at the edges of the leaf. Allow the paint to dry before proceeding to the next step.

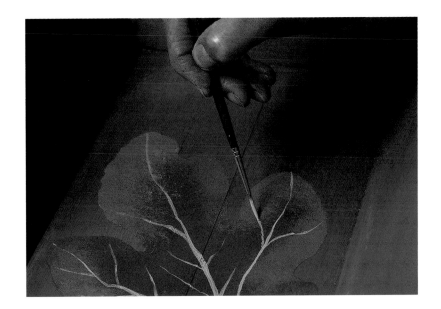

11 Add more white to the light green. With a medium stencil brush, stipple this over the leaf to add texture. Repeat steps 6–11 for the other two fig leaves.

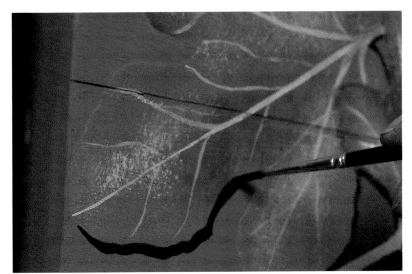

12 Using undiluted Payne's gray paint and the long, fine artist's brush, carefully paint the shadow around each of the leaves, remembering to take into account the direction of the imaginary light source, and not painting the shadows all the way around.

13 Use the same method as described in step 12 to paint subtle shadows in Payne's gray around each of the butterflies. When the paint is dry, varnish the whole basket with a hard-wearing product such as marine varnish, which will make it waterproof and suitable for outdoor use. Allow the first coat to dry completely before applying a second coat.

This very simple, chunky window box has been given an extra dimension with a trompe l'oeil fretwork pattern. Fretwork – ornament done with a scroll saw (fretsaw) – is found around the globe, often adorning the simplest of wooden houses.

Window Box

Here, the clever use of shadows creates a similar effect. Painting with shades of gray and cream, as has been done here, is a classic trompe l'oeil technique, and also makes a good background for flowers. However, if you prefer, you can give the window box a different look by changing to bright colors such as pinks and blues for a Caribbean look.

YOU WILL NEED
Window box

Woodstain: mid-gray

Stencils: fretwork design, shadows

Acrylic paint: cream or off-white, Payne's gray

Brushes: household paintbrush; small and medium stencil brushes; fine artist's brush; varnishing brush

Polyurethane varnish

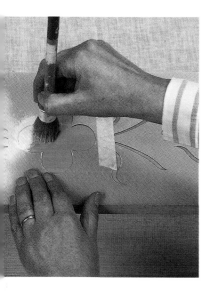

1 First paint the window box with two coats of a gray woodstain, using a household paintbrush. When the woodstain is completely dry, place the main stencil on the window box front, so that the cloverleaf motif is in the very center. Make sure that it is also centered vertically. Using a medium stencil brush, stencil the main part of the design (i.e., not the thin windows, which are for the shadows) in cream or off-white acrylic. When it is dry, you may need to stencil another coat, in order to cover the base coat.

2 Now turn the stencil around and reposition it so the cloverleaf motif is over the already stenciled one at the center of the window box. Stencil the remainder of the main part of the design in the same way. Do not remove the stencil.

Hints

Accurate stencil-cutting is essential here, so that the shadows fit exactly around the motif. The design is symmetrical in both directions, so you can turn the main stencil around rather than turning it over when stenciling the second half of the window box. The shadows, however, are not symmetrical at all, so they have to be done as two separate sections.

3 Use a small stencil brush and a mix of cream and Payne's gray to stencil the shadows onto the part of the window box that you stenciled in step 1. Remove the stencil. Now put the other (shadows) stencil over what you stenciled in step 2. Stencil these shadows in the same color.

4 Remove the shadows stencil. There will probably be a few gaps between the shadows and the main motif, so these gaps will need to be carefully touched up by hand, using a fine artist's brush and the same color of paint.

Style Ideas

Fretwork, sometimes called gingerbread, often takes the form of scrolls, curves, or other openwork that appears on door and window frames, porches, and other architectural features. All of these sources could provide inspiration for designs for this type of project.

5 With the same fine artist's brush, hand-paint a darker, narrower shadow to the left of each existing shadow, using Payne's gray (not mixed with white this time). When dry, varnish the window box.

Delft Tiles 12-15

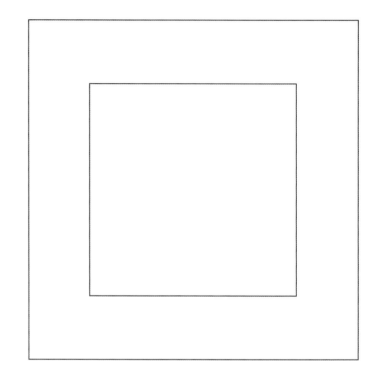

Card Table 16-21

Fire Screen 22-27

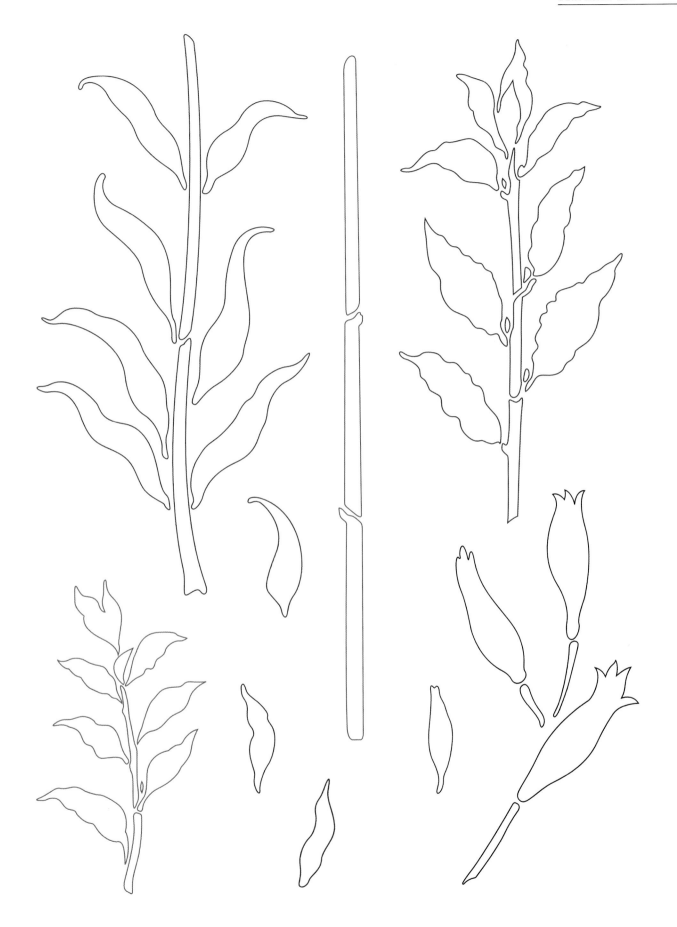

Marquetry Tray 28-31

Scagliola Table 32-37

French Plate 56-59   Ribbon Mirror 42-45

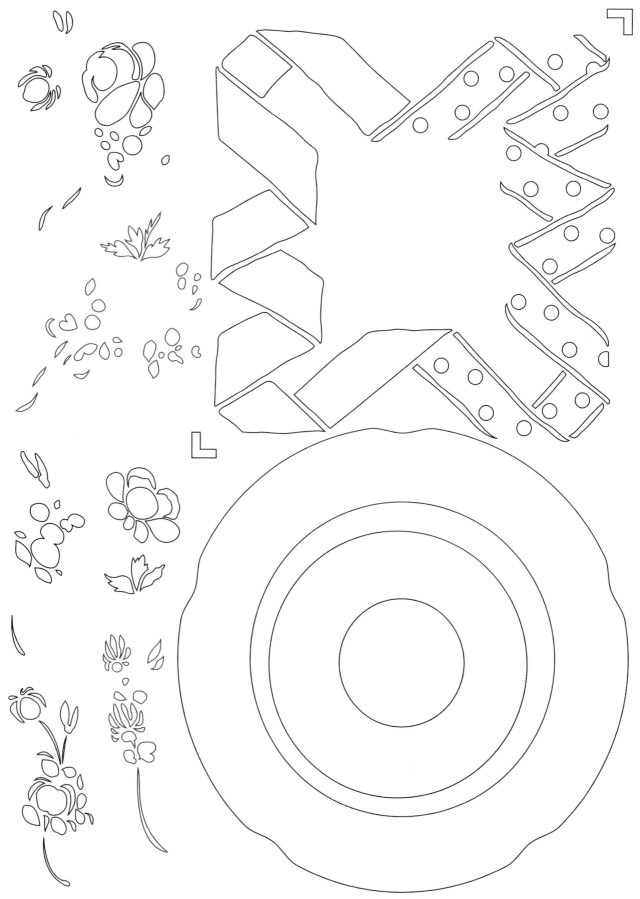

Simple Mural 50-55

Kilim Rug 60-65

Bathroom Cabinet 66-71

Stenciled Curtain

Texan Chest 72-77

Indian Print Blind
82-85

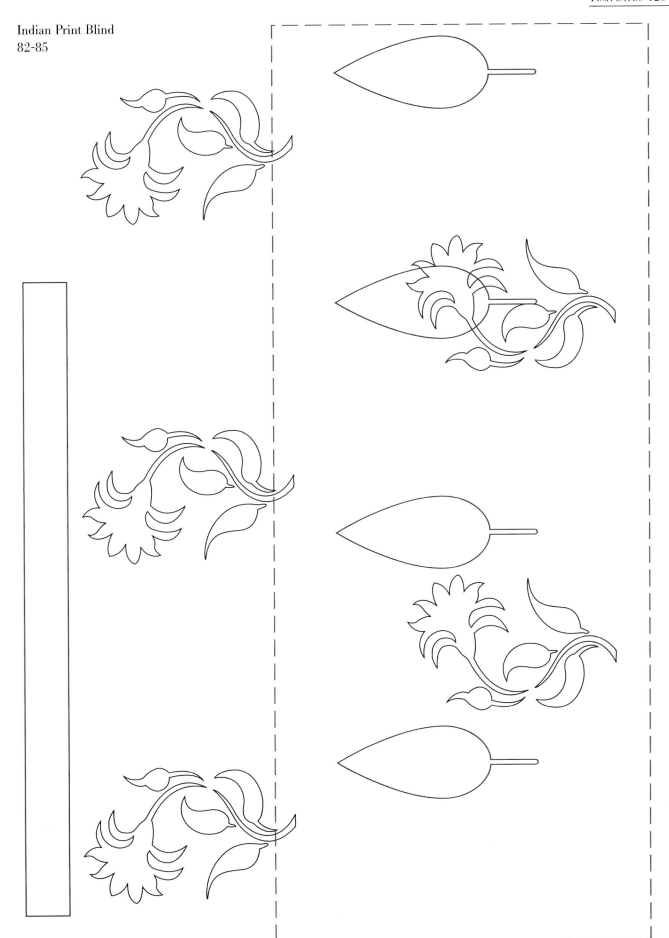

Stenciled Curtain 86-93

Garden Basket 104-109

Window Box 110-113